NOW IS YOUR TIME

A no bullsh!t guide for dreamers and doers

BY STEPH GOLD

COPYRIGHT

DISCLAIMER

Cover & Interior Design: Heidi Miller

Editing: Kate Makled

Author's photo courtesy of the author.

DEDICATION

Mom, thank you for always modeling the
utmost strength, determination, and work ethic.
Dad your unmatched positivity and support
will follow me throughout my journey.
Thank you both endlessly for always encouraging
me and helping me make my dreams a reality.
I love you both dearly.

TABLE OF CONTENTS

FOREWORD

I met Steph in sunny California at my retreat, The Bliss Project. When she described her initiative I knew instantly this was something I wanted to be a part of. Her message is beyond valuable and coming at an ideal time for young Dreamers. Millennials realize there has to be more to life than a nine to five with two weeks vacation a year. In the last few years we have witnessed an app putting cab companies out of business, with the creation of Uber. We have also witnessed an app putting hotel companies out of business with the birth of ARBNB. This generation is experiencing first hand how connected we all are with social media, free long distance, the world wide web, live streaming videos, and the ability to communicate face to face with people on the other side of the world thanks to Skype and Facetime.

Millennials are witnessing a major shift in the way we do business today and will be doing it in the future. They are realizing anything is possible and as freeing as that idea is it can also be incredibly crippling. It is easy to become overwhelmed with ideas in a world that is so abundant. Brilliant minds are graduating college and stalling, not for lack of drive, nor laziness but simply an overwhelm in possible direction. Their path has been lit up to college graduation and once they graduate their once illuminated path disappears into darkness. Not knowing where to turn many of these young dreamers are spinning their wheels.

Steph is finding these dreamers like you and holding a lantern so you can see your path. She is on a mission to mentor and guide millennials in a loving yet, motivating way to push them into action. It has become so easy to sit and wait, doubt, and spin ones wheels with little to no action.

How many thirty, forty, and even fifty year olds have you met whose dreams, mission, purpose, and passion have yet to be executed? Are you willing to be one of them?

In Now Is Your Time Steph will captivate you and ignite a fire so you begin acting on your purpose NOW. And watch out, because in the following pages you will find exercises to force you into action, even before you finish reading! This book provides real concrete steps to uncovering and living out your calling from the universe, immediately. Before you make a bunch of twists, turns, and excuses that will ultimately waste your time and stall you from impacting the world, take the action Steph lays out here.

Can you imagine a world where everyone spent their time in a career they truly loved, one they were absolutely confident was making a difference in the world, a job they were proud of?

This book will help dreamers like you navigate your way in this new unknown territory but you need to read the book and take action to get out of your own way and to your ideal life quickly.

There will never be a "right" time or "perfect" time to do something out of your comfort zone. Sometimes all we need is someone to push us out of the nest and what I love about this book is that it can help you do just that.

Your wildest dreams are possible and Steph is showing you the way, NOW!

Lori Harder
LIFESTYLE COACH & SELF LOVE EXPERT

INTRODUCTION

Welcome! My name is Steph Gold. I am a life coach, mentor, and advocate for recent female college graduates. I have been a life coach since 2011. I have worked with clients of all genders, ages, and reasons for seeking coaching. My focus over the last few years has been women experiencing a so-called quarter-life crisis. The majority of my clients have been between the ages of twenty-eight and thirty-two. I really enjoyed working with this age group, their reasons for contacting me were very similar as it became incredibly easy to predict the areas of their lives they would want assistance. When asked why they called me, the answer usually sounded like: "I want to lose weight." "I want to find the man of my dreams." "I want to be happy."

After a few short months of working with me, many shifts would happen with my clients. I coached countless breakups, weight loss journeys, cases of increased energy, new career paths, friendship shifts, surfacing of new hobbies, changes in living situation, and one client's process of moving across the country. I was loving the experience of "graduating" clients, saying farewell to changed women who would leave our final session with a new set of eyes on the world — and an obvious increase in their happiness and overall health and well-being. I could see the impact I was making on my clients, and I was loving introducing my peers to the effective and life-changing tools I learned, so they could use and carry with them throughout their entire lives.

It was a fulfilling career, however, one day it hit me. You know the way all great ideas do...like a ton of bricks. These great kinds of ideas like to show up just when you think you have figured out the world and finally things are starting to become predictable and effortless. What if I could find these clients five to nine years earlier? Just after college — before they choose the job they aren't really passionate about, the career that was suggested to them, passed down to them, determined for them, the first place to hire them or the just-for-the-moment job; the in-between job that helps stall the real world just long enough for them to remain comfortable and not have to deal with any real, big, or scary changes? What if I could find my clients before they stay in their college relationship, or with the first person they like well enough to tolerate for the next few years — or just long enough that the only thing keeping them together is the fear of being alone, never marrying or dying alone, because you know everyone that doesn't marry their college sweetheart dies alone (sarcasm)? What if I could find my client just out of college and give her the tools then — before she becomes overweight, miserable, desperate, and living a life built around excuses and lies. What if I could help her, before all of those crazy difficult things to undo occurred in the first place? How would I feel about my work then? The doer instead of the undoer...the guide as they figure out their best life now and spend their twenties living it...instead of the repairs department they consult on waking up miserable and wishing they could undo it all?

These young adults are ready to make decisions on their own, and they want to make their family, friends, professors, and ultimately their world proud. That is quite a bit of pressure when you have no guidebook (for the first time in your life).

The truth is you can totally figure this out. Your IQ does not matter, brilliant people have figured it out and so have the kids with the lowest GPA. There is no set time it will take you to figure it out on your own. Some take longer than others. For my recent clients, they only spent a few job changes, a couple long-term relationships, a few sets of awful friends, most of their twenties, about 25 lbs, and an average of about $10,000 worth of lessons to figure out they needed some help. Some marry the man or woman out of fear, have two to three kids, and confront the gap in their forties, and then realize they may need some guidance. I've had those clients too.

My point is you can totally do this on your own — that is, make a bunch of crazy twists and turns, hit countless dead ends and turn arounds, and ultimately get to an uncomfortable amount of lost before you realize you could use some guidance. Or you could recognize that up to this point, the road has been lit for you with very little possibility or potential for error — but now you've hit a spot on the road that isn't illuminated, and you can either feel your way around in the dark for as long as it takes you to finally ask for help, or you could stop and ask someone to hold your hand through this part with their flashlight to guide you until your path is lit again. I've seen it play out both ways and both totally lead you down the same path, there are no mistakes or accidents on this path of life. I will share with you this little secret…asking for help now gets you to your end goal a whole hell of a lot quicker.

I wrote this book for the individuals that have recently graduated and are trying to figure out life without a guidebook. During that time in our lives, everyone seems to have an opinion on what we should be doing or how we should be living. "You should be a counselor," I can recall my mom suggesting. "You should work at this not-for-profit I am on the board of," I heard countless individuals suggest. It is not that any of the suggestions I was receiving were bad — they just simply were not right *for me*. Trying to figure out what was *right* for me took me years. I tried so many different tools and ideas to get there quicker, and ultimately if I had known what I know now, I could have spent the last five years *actually doing* what I love and making a difference instead of researching, training, networking, and doing a lot of talking about how to make a difference and taking very little action. Now that I know the steps it takes to uncover an individual's passion, and aid him or her in strategizing a plan and executing it, I am determined to help.

I have found that working closely with other like-minded individuals can be a huge asset. I also know the important role our peers play in our lives at any age, but especially so as we are coming into our own just after college graduation. This is why I hold group calls, trainings, and retreats.

I know the importance of each individual realizing he or she is not alone in this journey, and seeing firsthand that someone else has the same concerns and questions that she does. It is also essential that these women experience and share successes *and* setbacks in order to help one another grow and support each other. When a client comes to me, the first thing we do together is a set of exercises and assessments to uncover a list of talents, strengths, gifts, and true joys of the individual. I then take her through a process to uncover her purpose. Once we identify the thing that will make her most happy, we surface every reason or excuse that she believes that results in a chance she will not execute this vision. I will tell you these are so unique to each individual and creative as well as complex. I have found that the more intelligent the individual, the more complex and intricate the excuses will be. I was a professional buyer and seller of excuses in my mid-twenties myself, so uncovering excuses, reasons their potential isn't being met — and other life factors for which my client is choosing a life of unhappiness as opposed to fulfillment — happens to be one of my favorite parts of my job.

Once we have identified every "reason" that could continue to pop up in the future, every justification as to why this individual is choosing a life of less satisfaction than their destiny, we then dive deeply into the science of happiness. I present concrete and scientifically proven explanations as to why many people will turn to unhealthy coping mechanisms of self-sabotage during times of confusion. I then step the individual through a series of tactics and tools he or she can easily implement into his or her daily life to avoid such destructive behaviors. I have a clear and easy-to-understand system that I have seen help others navigate their paths clearly and with such determination that they are now living the lives they deserve to live.

Now that you know who I am, who I work with, and have a little insight into my approach — let's dive deeper! I will caution you...the later chapters of this book contain exercises that include your participation. Once you have done the work, you won't be able to unsee what you've uncovered. So, if you want to stay small and continue to live a mediocre life, stop reading now.

CHAPTER 1

COLLEGE DOES A SHITTY JOB OF PREPARING YOU FOR LIFE AFTER GRADUATION

Spring has passed. Summer has gone. Winter is here...and the song I meant to sing remains unsung. For I have spent my days stringing and unstringing my instrument.

RABINDRANATH TAGORE

Think for a moment: What would the world look like if everyone spent their time doing something they truly loved, a career they were absolutely confident was making a difference in the world, a job they were proud of?

I know for me hours can go by in the blink of an eye when I am doing something I love to do. I think we all realize this and that is why we so often hear these words from our parents, "Do what you love," or, "Do what makes you happy." Those are great words of wisdom, but they are also crippling. While we agree that of course everyone wants to do something he or she loves to do, how are we supposed to know at such a young age, without experience, what it is that we will love so deeply that we will lose track of time? There is no map, no outline for what will give us this feeling of satisfaction or gratitude. What we often *do* know is what won't make us happy — giving up working twelve to eighteen hours a week with three months of summer vacation, plus almost one month around the holidays, a week at spring break — and trading that in for a 40-plus-hour work weeks with two vacation weeks a year.

Up until we graduate from college, the majority of our life decisions are structured for us. After grade school, it is understood that one will attend middle school, then high school, after that he or she will choose a college. Once in college, many have the freedom to choose how to spend the majority of their time. College is similar to high school but not exactly. In high school, our days are made up of school the same seven hours a day as everyone else — the only real choices are, do you participate in after-school activities or sports and which ones? If so, then afterward it's home for homework, dinner, and bed, only to wake up the next day and do it all over again.

After graduation, many kids leave the family home and are invited to make all kinds of decisions on their own: where to live, who to live with, going from at least thirty-five hours each week completely accounted for to twelve to eighteen hours a week in class with all their other time discretionary. Much experimentation occurs during these four precious learning years with all this newfound freedom, some new responsibilities, perhaps continuing allowance money from Mom and Dad, and the influence of our peers.

For four years, we live where we want, we decorate how we want, we clean or don't clean when we want, we drink when we want, we study or don't study when we want...there is no one to tell us what to do or when to do it. We are our own bosses and we make all the decisions. Sure, there are consequences if we don't study or complete our commitments — but basically we can figure out how to get by doing the bare minimum because ultimately we want the freedom to live the most fun and enjoyable life possible. For those who experience college with a generous allowance from Mommy and Daddy, life can be even more enjoyable. If we need more money, all we need to do is ask. Not work harder, *just ask*. Even better, we can make up a great excuse as to how the money ran away from our wallets and we need more for our basic needs: food, water, shelter, maybe class or books.

Ah, yes...over a four-year period of time, it seems we have finally mastered the good life. We know exactly how to work the least possible amount and spend the majority of our time living however we want. Our best version of our life, filled with fun, adventure, carefree shopping, day drinking and partying, dress-up parties, and so much more. We work to stay on track to graduate in four years, because we know that as long as we are on track and make acceptable grades, our parents will stay off our backs. After four years of freedom and the most fun of our lives, the Chancellor hands us a diploma — and life as we know it ends.

Our entire lives, we have been told what is coming next, and guided to the next step. Not now. Now it's on us. At least before now maybe we had to make a decision on which high school to attend or which college, some don't even have those decisions. Regardless, the bottom line is that we knew we were going to be going to school and we had an idea of what that would look like, what our day would be comprised of, but not now. Now we can literally do anything.

So open-ended, too open-ended — and for those who have not had to take on these responsibilities before, such a massive decision to make can be completely crippling. We turn to our parents for guidance, but if you have parents like mine they are saying unhelpful and wildly ambiguous things like, "Do what makes you happy." Awesome. What makes me happy? What does that look like? Can I get paid to stay in college and never work for my money? *I know, I will prolong my decision by going back to school, because that's what I know and that's where I am safe. I will justify it with an excuse like, "Well, in order to do X, I need my Masters in Y."* For some, they know exactly what they want and going to medical school or law school *is* the logical next step, super stoked for those people — but those individuals aren't me, and they aren't my clients. For myself and the majority of my clients, this newfound freedom just might become absolutely paralyzing.

The expectations others have of a recent college graduate are high, and no one seems to shy away from the question, "What's next?" Worse, they do not seem too timid to attempt to direct you, "You know what you should do? (enter one of the million random suggestions people come up with here)." Most of the time those interactions are easy to navigate, especially when you don't really know the individual making the suggestion, so you are pretty easily able to brush it off. What if the suggestion is coming from someone you love and respect, someone who knows you better than anyone else, and is invested in the outcome? It could be someone who just paid for four years of college for you, like a parent or grandparent. It could be another family member or your best friend's family, who has also given you at least a lot of emotional support. Those words of advice are more difficult to turn down because they know us, and we feel watched. Maybe we are also feeling guilty for being confused or stalling ambition, because we have a sense that we owe them to make something of ourselves. Lots of guilt, lots of stress, and then of course there is the confusion and fear itself.

Maybe their suggestion is perfectly reasonable, but it came from them, and not from within us, so we are in resistance. Remember, I have been calling the shots for the last four years, I have been making all my decisions, I have been encouraged to dream bigger — and now I am supposed to give up my power and revert back to the way things were before? I have grown. I am an adult. No thanks for the suggestion, Mom and Dad. I will make this one on my own.

We consider our options, most require much more of our free time than we are willing to give up. I'm sorry — you want me to go from working twelve to eighteen hours a week to forty hours a week? You want me to trade in three months off during the summer, a month at the holidays, and spring break for two weeks' vacation? *Have you lost your mind? I am young. I am craving adventure! I want to see the world! What I need is to find a job where I work a little, make enough to pay the bills and satisfy my parents, maintain my freedom, all while figuring this all out.* If you are like me, you don't just have one idea on how you can accomplish your goals and make an impact — and there is no road map for you. Your vision is bigger, different, something else…some layout that society has yet to discover, or at least fully integrate. I can tell you what happens while you network, dream, create vision boards, tell others, journal about your true passion and all your goals. In the meantime, while you take the part time job to plan your future — you know, until "the time is right" or you are "ready" — we choose mediocrity. Basically, we take the easy road while we "figure it out" and waste years doing so.

I have watched many individuals, including myself, waste so much time planning a perfect execution of their vision. In the meantime, life continues to pass you by, your excuses become more abundant — and so involved, that even you are not able to identify them. Instead, you'll interpret them as factual things, people, and events that are holding you back, standing in the way of what you really want. You will be too close to it to understand that the only obstacle in your way of utter bliss is your own thoughts.

I think this issue can be best illustrated through real-life examples. Take Morgan, for example. Beautiful girl, graduated in less than four years in 2007 from Mizzou. Her passion was singing, music, managing others... She is a doer, go-getter, a game changer, and one of the hardest workers I've ever met. After she graduated she did the next logical thing and started working in sales. She was taught by others and society that money and power would make her happy — not singing or making a difference — so she started grinding. Driven to make money, she was killing it. She buried herself in work. Making a lot of money, she was putting much away in savings. She made enough to buy a beautiful home, and furnish it with top designer products and quality furniture. She maintained her college romantic relationship and in that regard was safe. She could buy anything she wanted and she had a man locked down. She was set.

I met Morgan at a real estate function while I was supporting my dear friend, who happened to be her realtor, and she asked what I did. When I said "life coaching," she immediately replied, "I need one!" I laughed (thinking, why on earth would this chick need me? She has everything), to which she replied, "I'm not happy and I don't know why." A lot of young women, I learned, feel the same way, although they may not articulate it the same way as Morgan did.

At our first appointment, I assessed her life. The girl was clean as hell, amazing job, long-term boyfriend... *Hmm.* I was puzzled, so I asked what areas of her life she would like to change. She said her weight and overall happiness

— so I began weight-loss coaching her. Week two brought nothing lost, not even an inch. Week three and still nothing changed. I fired her as a weight-loss client then, and said, "For some reason, this weight is serving a purpose for you. You don't want to lose weight for some reason and we need to get to the bottom of *that*. It's something deeper."

Once we identified weight as one of her excuses for not living her ideal life, we were one step closer. After a few weeks of diving in deeply to her thoughts and true passion, we were making headway. She executed the tools and steps brilliantly — and within a few months, we had a whole new plan. Morgan quit her successful career because it wasn't her passion, she broke up with the boyfriend (who incidentally turned out to be living a double life and had another serious girlfriend...umm creeper), then she moved out of her home and across the country.

The minute she began managing an upcoming artist — and living her purpose, that of managing and helping others with a hand in music — everything began to fall into place! She was happy...and a few dress sizes smaller, I might add. It's no coincidence that when we stop believing our excuses, like "I need to lose weight," our excuses start to disappear. We create our own reality.

I'll give you another example. When I turned 28, I decided I would spend the year making a serious effort to try new things. I was determined to try new foods, see new places, have new experiences, and meet new people. I called this yearlong challenge "365 new things," and you can check out some of the fun I got myself into on Instagram: #365Goldsnewthings. This challenge allowed me to put myself out there in ways I never could have imagined. It was so beneficial and enjoyable that I have decided to continue to live in the way it invited me to, even after my challenge year ended.

While making a serious effort to put myself out there, I met this incredible young woman. I was headed to Long Boat Key for my dear friend Christina's bachelorette party. I have a friend, Nikki, who I met while studying abroad. She lives in Fort Lauderdale, which is a little over an hour from Long Boat, so I decided to fly in a day early, rent a car, stay a night with Nikki, and then drive to the bachelorette party. As part of my 365-day challenge, I tried to uncover something unique about the place I was traveling, and see what activity or food adventure I needed to make happen while away.

During my investigation, I came across what is called the Mangrove tunnels. Kayaking or paddle boarding seemed to be the only way to experience these tunnels. I had been kayaking countless times before and had never tried paddleboarding, so I called a paddleboard company and made a reservation for an early morning excursion prior to my expected arrival at the bachelorette party.

When I left Nikki's place early that morning, I had no idea how incredible and life-changing an experience I was about to have. I reached Sarasota and drove down a narrow gravel road and down a short path, passing a few adventure crews carrying kayaks and unloading snorkel gear from their trucks. I found a place to park right up front. As I was unloading my car, this sporty, fit, pretty young blonde walked up and asked softly, "Steph?" "Yes!" I eagerly replied. "Hi, I am Pam," the sweet girl answered. She instructed me to leave everything in my car and follow her.

I can recall walking down the gravel path, paddleboard in hand, feeling so unsure and nervous about what I was about to do. She calmly instructed me on how to get on the board, and paddle out of the entry point so that others in line could enter the water. I can recall how nervous I was that I would not be able to balance and therefore look like a goofball in front of cute Pam and the hot adventure crew guys nearby. Thankfully, it was much easier than I had originally thought. I loved my first experience on the board. As we drifted off together toward the tunnels, Pam and I began to connect. How rare it was to have a private lesson with one of this company's instructors. How crazy that it would be Pam — and how incredibly grateful I am, that she felt comfortable enough with me to share her story while we were out.

Pam is a beautiful example of an intelligent woman who graduated college and followed everyone's suggestions perfectly in her early twenties. Pam had been valedictorian of her high school, a scholar-athlete, Silver Knight nominee, and always gave everything — from school to sports to family and friendships — 100% of her effort. People had big expectations for her. She graduated from the University of Florida with a master's degree in accounting. Afterward,

Pam passed the CPA exam, married her college sweetheart, moved to Norfolk, Virginia for his job, and found a reputable public accounting firm to launch her career. Pam thought she was finally in a position to "be happy." She had begun her career that she spent years building, was making good money, and was married to a great man who had a high-paying engineering job and was pleasant to be around. She *thought* she was living the dream. She had followed society's outline perfectly, she had done everything that society agreed with — so why on earth did she feel so unhappy?

Unsure of where to turn, since the booze and late-night partying weren't filling the void, she found yoga. She described to me how her accounting firm began offering yoga on Thursdays during lunch. She thought, *why not?* In class, she described a life-changing moment for her — when the instructor asked the participants to feel their feet on the ground...really feel their feet...all four corners of each foot grounded on the Earth at the same time. Pam explained that this moment, at the age of twenty-five, was the first time she had ever given any thought to the feeling of her feet on the ground. Thus Pam's beautiful journey of stepping into herself began. She found a place to be alone with Pam. She uncovered an opportunity to meditate and tap into her innermost feelings and desires. Pam fell in love with yoga, and began uncovering layers of herself. And since this "epiphany" moment, Pam knew it was her soul's duty to pass on this idea of living mindfully and consciously to younger women.

The more she attended yoga, the more intrigued she became, and went on to obtain her 200-hour Yoga Teacher Training (YTT) certificate. It was on the mat where she began to realize many areas of her life needed to be adjusted in order for her to be living out her purpose and most authentic life. Her yoga instructor became her mentor and she would hear her say things like, "We are not our thoughts, we have a truth underlying all of this." Pam told me that she would lie awake at night thinking something needed to change, knowing she wasn't happy, and there had to be more to life. She told me that once the voice started, she couldn't make it stop. The voice would ask questions like, "Did I get married because I wanted to get married, because that's what people do to be happy, or because I loved him?" She couldn't turn off the ringing in her head that said, "This isn't my truth."

She ran to her boss and told him she needed to quit, that there was something more to life and she had to find it. Her boss made the practical assumption that poor Pam just needed some time off, and graciously offered her a sabbatical from work and to return when she was ready. Pam walked out that day knowing she could never come back the same way. She told her husband that she thought they might need to end their marriage, and she left on a solo cross-country road trip. Pam traveled on a month-long camping trip across the US. She attended music festivals, historical sites and cultural events alone and began falling in love with herself. Pam began to explore her connection with nature, other people, and the idea that everything in life needs to work together. She returned to Norfolk with a fresh set of eyes on the world.

Ultimately, she and her husband decided to part ways. She also left her company's grueling full-time schedule, and began working from Florida. This transition to part-time and remote status not only gave her more time to develop her game plan, but also gave her the much needed space to go after her dreams of being her most authentic spiritual self, all the while not knowing what her next step would be. That's when she discovered paddleboarding and organic farming. She started an organic popcorn business, Peacecorn, and began traveling to festivals, concerts, and other social events to share her pop and her newfound understanding of growing organically. This not only aligned her more with her soul purpose, but also aligned her with like-minded, inspiring individuals. It was at one of these events that she was introduced to a volunteering opportunity at a nearby elementary school, and began teaching underprivileged children how to garden and the importance of eating real food.

Months into her new ventures she met a man. The right man. The Pam I met who was twenty-nine years old, growing organic non-GMO popcorn, giving back to her community through gardening and working with kids, teaching and leading paddleboard tours, along with empowerment workshops for young girls. This was an entirely different Pam than the married, miserable Pam living in Norfolk, Virginia, working insane hours at her accounting job, and living an unhappy life.

Once Pam was fed up with living an unfulfilling life, and decided no excuses would stand in her way of living her best life now, she began to design her ideal life and stopped living the life everyone else thought she should live. Pam is now a successful wellness coach living her *dream life*.

Both Morgan and Pam are examples of what so many young adults experience throughout the recent years following college graduation. I am currently six and a half years out of college, and I do not have a single friend that is with the same company they started with out of school. Sure, I have friends in the same general line of work, be it real estate, marketing, sales, banking, etc. In many cases, I have watched as friends and clients alike changed career paths entirely. This, of course, is a very different scenario than many of our parents are accustomed to. My father, for example, worked for the same company, in the same department, for thirty-nine years. My mother was a computer programmer from the time she graduated until she opened her own consulting company — and hired system engineers to work for her. The way business has changed over the last forty or so years, among other factors, plays a role in this evolution. Regardless of the reasoning, these differences present a divide in perspective among the generations as to how a career is built. This can result in the differing of opinions as to which career path to take, how long to stay at your first company, the appropriate order of things, etc.

The changing of entire careers in young adulthood can be by interpreted by the older generations as laziness, being fickle, having ADD, not allowing enough time to grow in the company, etc. The truth is, I don't believe this generation to be more lazy than generations past. Instead, I interpret the changing of careers and jobs by those in their twenties today to be the result of them realizing the world is a different place than it was forty years ago. Times have changed since men wore suits and ties every day and carried a briefcase to and from work. Travel agents were once needed, people who study brochures and pamphlets to learn about locations — now we have the World Wide Web, countless travel websites, and apps. The only way to get ahold of people a generation ago was their work or home phone. Today, we have unlimited long distance and cell phones that we carry with us at all times. The world of business is much more global and easy to access. It is no longer difficult to be working while at a remote location — or at all hours of the day and night. Business is evolving rapidly, and recent college grads realize this.

When I first graduated from college, I began dabbling in sales with a network marketing company. I still love the products and continue to follow many of the leaders of this company, as they are empowering, inspiring, and very motivating. There is a group that includes eighteen- to thirty-five-year-old sales associates of this company. When I began following this company, that group of individuals included seven people and now, just three short years later, contains over 50,000 people in that age range. I share this because it is extremely illustrative of what this generation is craving. What can a network marketing structure offer that most conventional career paths cannot? This generation is craving flexible hours, the ability to take vacation whenever one chooses, adventure, and fun fun fun! I believe the job switching and high turnover rate in so many workplaces is not a result of laziness but instead is a product of this generation realizing that there has to be an easier way. With the rise of technology and how connected we all are, there must be a way to have it all, with the freedom and financial backing... but what is it? There is no road map. It's hard to consult older generations (parents, grandparents) because they will tell you all about what they know...the path to success *for them* was to work a nine-to-five and get two weeks of vacation a year, wah wah wah. But, you know, just as I know, that there is something else. There *is* a way you can make the money and have as many vacation days as you want.

We might say we want flexibility of hours or more opportunity for travel, but the underlying truth is that ultimately we want the freedom to choose. We want to have the opportunity to live our lives the way we want to, and not be told how to spend our time. We think that freedom will give us happiness, but the truth is that the combination of living our purpose, knowing we are making a difference, having the opportunity to see and experience the beautiful world in which we live, and knowing and loving ourselves more fully is where happiness lives.

In Morgan's case, she was not happy working the conventional job because she was being motivated by money and living the life she thought was expected of her. Once she transitioned into a very unconventional career path, one that had no road map, she was happy because she knew she was making a difference in the lives of others. She woke up every morning driven to help this artist make it and ultimately enable him to make his dream a reality and support himself and his family. She is passionate and living with purpose. I don't know that she isn't working even harder and more hours than before but her efforts do not feel like "work." She is truly loving what she does and the life she is living.

Pam's case is not much different, she too thought she was doing everything right by marrying young, taking on a successful career, but she was miserable. Today, she loves life. She isn't making nearly as much money — but remember, it isn't wealth that drives happiness, it is living your purpose and seeing the impact you are making in the lives of others. The real problem is that college does not prepare you for life after college. We graduate and are then left helpless and wandering through the next few years trying to act like we totally have it all figured out, when the truth is very few of us actually do. I want everyone who graduates college to have the tools they need to get to their best life sooner than it took Morgan, Pam, and myself. Ready to hear my story and how I totally qualify to preach about this issue? Buckle up.

NOTES

NOTES

NOTES

CHAPTER 2

THIS IS BECAUSE OF MY CIRCUMSTANCE; I PLAYED NO PART

The beauty of life is, while we cannot undo what is done, we can see it, understand it, learn from it and change.

J. EDWARDS

You may wonder why I am confident that I am qualified to help college graduates. You may be questioning my experience. I will share with you my experience after college graduation, but in order to really understand me and where I am coming from, you must first learn a little about my life before I graduated.

WHERE IT ALL BEGAN

I was born in Saint Louis, Missouri to a teenage girl who had been shunned by her Catholic family because she was pregnant. She ran away from her family, and hid while keeping me safe, until I was born. Wanting the best life possible for me, she put me up for adoption upon my birth. The agency told my parents that they stayed in contact with her, and after she had given birth to me, she asked her parents for forgiveness and they took her back in. It was a closed adoption, so that is all the information I have. My birthmother was a badass warrior and really that's all I need to know to be inspired by her — and forever grateful to her for the life she gave me.

A month after my birth, I was adopted by the most incredible couple. My mother and father had wanted a child for six years before I arrived. They were unable to conceive a child on their own, and turned to adoption. Growing up, I celebrated the day of my birth and then a short month and one day later my Arrival Day, the day my parents picked me up from the agency. My father would tell the story of that day every year on my Arrival Day. He described how my parents had nothing for a baby in the house the morning they received the call to come pick up their baby girl. He would tell me how they rushed around buying diapers, a car seat, bottles, and formula. They were so excited, calling all their friends and family to come over to the house. They brought me home that day, and I was welcomed by a houseful of loving family and friends. I've watched the home videos from that day, and I am pretty confident my father had the camera rolling non-stop for twenty-four hours. He would describe that day as one of the happiest days of his life.

My parents were extremely successful in their careers. By the time I arrived, both my parents were in their late thirties. My mom owned her own computer consulting company. She is the most brilliant woman I have ever met.

She is beyond intelligent, the oldest of seven children. My mom had lost her mother in a car accident that my mother was also involved in. My mother was in critical condition, read her last rites at the age of fourteen, and a long six months later finally released from the hospital. My mom has strength unlike anyone I have ever encountered. From the age of fourteen on, my mom was raised by her widowed father. My grandfather was a brilliant businessman and started his own steel company that was a massive success.

My mom has always been the model of discipline, drive, strength, determination, and incredible work ethic. She is unstoppable and her brilliance commands respect. I love watching my mom speak to a group of individuals, especially men. I think often people underestimate the intelligence of a beautiful woman but her intelligent use of language makes her a poetic wordsmith. She also takes no shit from anyone, yet refuses to suffer fools in her own respectful and confident manner. She has always used complex words to mean simple things. Her diction and vocabulary are often confusing to me when we are having casual conversations. I've always loved to watch her work or speak about something she is passionate about. My mom usually gets what she wants, and that is because her passion and drive in combination with her intelligence are unmatched.

My father was the second oldest son in his family. My dad's mother, who my first book is based on, was a pioneer and trailblazer. She stayed at home and took incredible care of her four boys. My father's dad was a hard worker, an entertainer and entrepreneur. My father was born to do sales. My grandmother would describe how he, as a child on Halloween, would unload his bag of candy and line up each piece next to a like piece, all the Twix together, Hershey's, and so on — then he would sell his candy to other children. In college, my father made calendars and went around to local shops and sold ad space for the calendars. He then sold the calendars to students on campus. He was incredibly successful, and I believe one of his college buddies took over the business and continues to sell ads on creative media to this day (forty-plus years later).

After college, my father sold incentive travel at a company called Maritz, where he worked for thirty-nine years and grew from a travel agent, to director, to vice president of the department. People loved my dad. He was the kind of individual you never forgot. When he died, friends from kindergarten, high school, college — all stages of his life — came to pay respects at his memorial. People wrote letters expressing how his zest for life, perspective, and energy had made a lifelong impact on them. His positivity and enjoyment in the little things were unlike any individual I have ever met. My father loved life — and everyone and everything it had to offer him.

A tear ran down my cheek with every word I typed about my parents. Not because this makes me sad, but because that is how deeply I love these people. That is just how much they both mean to me — and in order to understand who I am you must first know a little about where I came from and who they are.

I was spoiled, of course. Two successful individuals finally have their prayers answered and what...you think they left me out in the cold? No, I had everything I ever wanted and more. I was loved and cared for so deeply. I had an incredible childhood. My parents were both beyond supportive of me. My father loved capturing life's moments, so naturally my family has enough video footage and photographs to fill a massive storage locker. He loved life, and us. Oh yes... *us*... So around the age of three, I began asking for a sibling. Well, you know how this story goes. My parents couldn't have biological kids. My parents told me to ask Santa, the Easter Bunny, to pray to Jesus...clearly, they were outsourcing my request. However, sitting on Santa's lap brought nothing but utter confusion as he would reply, "Better talk to your mommy and daddy about that one, little girl." I was accustomed to getting the things that I really wanted and I couldn't understand what the holdup was. Finally, a few months after I turned four, the best day of my life occurred... we received the call to come pick up my brother.

It was a special day, so I chose to wear my blue corduroy dress with the ABCs written all over it in bright colors, I had on bright red shoes to match, and a bright bow in my hair. I remember bringing him home. I wouldn't leave his side, after all he was mine, I was the one who had asked, prayed, and did everything within my power to get him. Months later, my parents took me to Mexico while baby Ryan stayed with grandma so they could explain to me that Ryan was not just mine, even though I had asked for him, but he was another member of the family. True story.

I loved my brother so much I never wanted to leave his side. Since I had pined for him for so long, I think I took ownership, responsibility for him in a way maybe similar to a feeling mothers do when they have children. I felt like my wishing, praying and hoping created my brother and therefore it was not until a couple years after college that I realized what I was doing and stopped taking ownership or responsibility for his actions. If you've never tried to control someone or something you have zero control over this will not make sense, however the burden I was placing on myself to keep him safe from all harm and influence him to make the best decisions, was overwhelming. I would even attempt to discipline him in front of my parents. I can recall my mother saying, "Stephanie, I am right here." I think part of that was the fact that my parents both worked full-time, so we had many different babysitters over the years. I always felt like regardless of which adult was in charge, my brother and I were a team, and that it was ultimately *my* job to keep him safe and out of trouble, since I was the one constant.

Reflection:

Being born of a warrior, adopted into an incredible family with two successful parents that provided for me so generously definitely contributed to the amount of pressure I put on myself to make them proud. I did this because my love and appreciation for everything they had done for me was so great. Looking back, I am able to see patterns that started at a very young age with my brother. I realize now looking back how I took ownership of his behavior and mistook my role of sister, for second mother, from the very beginning.

QUESTIONS FOR REFLECTION:

- What is your family life like?

- Who were the individuals in your family that inspired you at a young age?

- Describe the best day of your life as a child...do you remember what you were wearing? What made it so special?

* * *

NOTES

THE SCHOOL DAYS

I attended a private co-ed Catholic grade school from kindergarten to eighth grade. In grade school, I took dance classes, and played volleyball, soccer, basketball, and softball. I was on the swim team at our country club in the summers and took tennis lessons there, too. I was in Girl Scouts, and sold hundreds of boxes of Girl Scout cookies every year. This happened partly because I wasn't afraid to make phone calls, knock on people's doors, and ask for the sale — but mostly because both my parents would also take my form to their offices. I also remember being one of the school's top wrapping paper salesmen, which was mostly due to the same reasons, also in part because I learned there was this pretty eccentric lady who lived a couple houses down who was obsessed with wrapping paper. My sales really took a dive after she moved. I played piano for years but was never really great at it. I didn't practice much and I can recall one of my last piano lessons, my parents had hired a young male to teach me, I was fifteen at the time. I would get excited for my lessons because I was a little boy crazy and we would sit and talk for the majority of the lesson. My dad poked his head out of the kitchen one night, about twenty minutes into my lesson, and said, "I don't hear any playing going on." It wasn't long after that I stopped taking lessons.

After grade school, I went to a private all-girls high school. I knew some of the girls from the country club and another athletic club my family belonged to. I remember trying out for volleyball and not making the team my freshman year.

The only "walk-on" sport was track, so freshman year, I ran track. I was horrible. I can remember trying to plea with opponents only to beat me by a little at the end, so I wasn't the last one running far behind.

After playing sports my entire life, I was pretty crushed to realize that phase of my life might be over. I spent the next couple years basically being told I wasn't good enough. The school exempted me from taking a foreign language because they said I had a learning disability that would prohibit me from being able to learn another language. I was pretty miserable at this school. It wasn't the girls, or the teachers, but I think it was that I wasn't involved in any outside activities. My personality — and all that I had to offer — wasn't able to shine in that environment. I had lost my sense of purpose and I was miserable. I became angry and depressed. I can recall my parents looking across the table at me one evening, during dinner, and staring at me with a look of utter shock and confusion after I had gone on some angry rant. My mother said, "Where did our happy girl go?" My dad followed up with, "Yes, I think you need to go to your room and figure out what is going on." When I finally entered the world again, after hours of deep contemplation, I told my parents I needed to switch schools.

I can remember touring what would soon be my new school. It was a co-ed, non-religiously affiliated private school. The only two rules in the school were "be nice" and "do the right thing." All the classes were small, with only twelve students to a room, and the teachers sat at tables with the students as they taught. My first year at my new school, I played both volleyball and soccer. All the sports were walk-on, and although I wasn't good at them, I loved being a part of the team and was the best cheerleader on the bench. That year, I attended a ceremony where the administrators present awards to members of the student body in front of the school for various reasons. I can recall sitting in the audience and telling myself, "I am going to win an award next year." I knew one sure way was to play three sports, and qualify for the "Tri-Star Athlete Award." Easy enough...I decided to try out for the cheerleading squad. Oh my gosh, you have never seen a more uncoordinated cheerleader in your life. I decided at the end of my first year to run for president of the student body. I can recall writing my speech and rehearsing with my mom. She cautioned me not to get my hopes up, as I had only been at the school a year, and many of the other candidates had attended the school since middle school. I took note of her advice, but did not seem to allow it to hold me back. I was completely comfortable with whatever outcome awaited — and was excited for the opportunity to speak in front of the entire school.

Long story short, I was elected by the student body to be president of the school. In my senior year, I found an excuse to stand up in front of the student body every morning and give some type of announcement. I was so comfortable and confident on stage. I look back on some of the things I did or said back then and can't believe it was me. One day, I can even recall singing "I'm a Survivor" by Destiny's Child into the mic at all-school announcements, just to cheer up the volleyball team after a loss the day before. I was so incredibly happy and in my element during senior year. I felt completely comfortable being myself and felt like I could accomplish anything in that supportive environment. I woke up every morning elated to go to school. I would arrive at least a half an hour before school started each day. Many days I was one of the first students to arrive and one of the last to leave. I stayed after school most days because of my after-school sports.

I can recall receiving my final report card and it had a sticker on the front that said "Dean's List." My mom pointed it out, and I immediately pulled the paper from her hand and responded, "Oh this must have been a mistake, I will tell them tomorrow." It wasn't a mistake. The last report card of high school I had the best grades I had ever had. This was also the year I was able to dedicate a few months to volunteering with an urban arts program and had the ability to work with underprivileged students in my community. I could see the impact I was making and my soul was full of love for these students. At the end of the year it was award ceremony time. I knew I would receive the Tri-Star Athlete Award...that was a given. My parents gathered and sat in the audience. I can remember the feeling when my coach called my name and the crowd cheered. It felt amazing to accomplish my goal. I sat back down in my chair and then heard my name a second time! This time my volleyball, cheerleading, and soccer coaches were awarding me the Coaches' Award. This award was not given to me for being the best athlete — and that was obvious —

but instead being a "memorable and important part of the team." I spent a lot of time yelling encouraging things from the bench and clearly that did not go unnoticed. Finally, the third time my name was announced, it was by the head of school who was awarding me an award he noted he had created just for me. It was called the "President's Leadership Award." In front of everyone, he proclaimed how proud he was to see my growth, dedication, and involvement in the school in just one year. I was beyond touched and deeply moved. I knew in that moment that I was in the place I belonged. I had found a place where I was understood and so were my efforts. I remember hugging my parents after the event. The look on their faces was priceless and so fulfilling. My dad was beaming with pride and my mother's eyes glistened and face was flushed from crying tears of joy. The feeling of making them proud was indescribable, and it will never leave me. Achieving that feeling of pride from them became a driving force that would continue to push me throughout my college and career life.

As I moved on to college, I had all the tools I needed to be successful. The awards and success achieved in my last year in high school were enough to propel me into college with serious confidence and desire for involvement. In my freshman year I joined a sorority, and throughout college was incredibly active in the house. I held numerous leadership positions. I was a residential advisor while living in the house. I held a position on the governing body that oversees all the sororities, the Panhellenic Council, and served as their vice president of events. In that position,

I hired motivational speakers to come and speak to all of the students involved in campus sororities and fraternities. Outside of sorority involvement, I was also a member of the Chancellor's Leadership Program. In order to hold your position in this elected group of individuals, you were required to meet an incredible amount of requirements each semester. Community service was essential, and influenced my involvement as a leader of LEAPs — which was a campus-wide initiative of an entire day of service to the Fort Worth community. In order to graduate from the Chancellor's Leadership Program, each student was required to develop a project that they would present to the chancellor. One requirement of this project was that it needed to make a positive impact on the community. For my project, I decided to travel back to my high school and present a presentation on internet safety. As a result of the feedback I received from the high school and staff, in regards to enjoyment and effectiveness of my presentation, I really began to develop my love for public speaking.

In college I majored in Communications, with an emphasis in Human Relations and minored in Psychology of Leadership. My workload and coursework allowed me to constantly reflect on what makes people individuals and how to effectively empower others. I took countless writing emphasis courses in college and as a result was constantly writing many more papers than I was taking exams. I was also giving speeches on various topics from class at least monthly. I was quickly learning that I loved public speaking and writing dearly.

While I was away at school, living in Texas, the dynamic of my family life back home was beginning to change. My entire family drove me to school my freshman year and helped me move into the dorms. My father had just decided to start working from home and travel less. I remember feeling jealous that my brother would have so much of father's attention while I was gone...looking back now I am grateful they were given that bonding time. So I am a freshman in college, after my senior year in high school I am feeling awesome. I am riding the high, life is perfect and everything is happening exactly as it's meant to. My family drops me off in August and drives home. That first semester while I am learning the ropes in Texas my family is bonding and growing extremely close.

REFLECTION:

Being told "no, you aren't good enough, you aren't athletic enough, you aren't smart enough" by adults I respected was difficult to overcome as a child. It did, however, allow me the opportunity to learn at a young age how losing one's sense of purpose can quickly spiral into a tornado of depression. Switching schools taught me to change scenery and take chances: I might not be the best but I joined the team, put myself out there, and tried something new. Feeling my parents pride on Awards Day propelled me into a subconscious obsessive need for their approval beyond anything else. When you feel the pride of someone you love deeply, it is easy to dedicate your efforts to achieving that feeling again. In college, I was reminded that staying involved and continuing to try new things can help cultivate one's strengths and allow them to become aware of their gifts and passion.

QUESTIONS FOR REFLECTION:

- What hobbies did you have as a child? What did you *love* to do?

- Can you recall areas where you stood out or excelled as a child?

- Were you ever told you weren't good enough by someone you respected? A teacher, a parent, a coach? How did you handle it?

* * *

NOTES

THINGS TAKE A TURN

At the time, my father's newly flexible schedule was enabling him to drive my brother to and from school. The two developed a close bond and friendship. Every time I called home to check in, I was caught up on everything I was missing out on back home. My brother and father went on a ski trip, they bought and rode dirt bikes together, they even started taking guitar lessons. That fall, my parents went on a romantic getaway that was long overdue due to their crazy work schedules. I can recall coming home that first Christmas and thinking everything was perfect. After I was accepted into the sorority, my father even surprised me at our first banquet. He had flown down and was awaiting my arrival when the elevator doors opened into the dining hall of the hotel where our welcome ceremony was being held. I remember the sheer joy of seeing him arrive and having him physically present to support me. Yes, fall semester of 2005 my world was perfect...too perfect. I didn't know the wrench that was about to be thrown into my family's lives. Even if I had, there is no way I ever could have planned for the next nine years of immense growth that awaited me.

The second semester of my freshman year, my mom came to visit for a work conference. We went to lunch and while catching me up on everything back home my mom also informed me that my father had fainted in church the previous Sunday. She said they left church and Dad slept it off and seemed to be better. I felt super uneasy about that story. Nothing like that had ever happened. My dad had never been sick a day in his life. I called my dad and told him I had heard about Sunday's events. I assured him that simply hearing that he was fine was not enough for me, and that I would call him back in thirty minutes and wanted to know when his appointment was. Sure enough, he made a doctor's appointment for Friday. The doctor informed my father that he was severely anemic and that he was suspicious my dad might have leukemia. The doctor sent the test results to a lab and told my dad he would know for sure the following Monday. At the nail salon on Friday, my mother received a call from my dad informing her of the news. I can still hear the concern in her voice as she spoke to him: "That's not good. Oh Rick. That's not good." I began calling out from the massage chair in the back of the little shop, "Mom, what's wrong? What is it?"

In an effort to protect me from unnecessary worry, my mother told me that my father was anemic and would be fine. I knew a few iron pills would solve that, so every ounce of worry disappeared. That Sunday was the day of the Super Bowl. I was waiting for the family I babysat for to pick me up, and meanwhile decided to call home and check in. It was a beautiful sunny day as I stood on my dorm's front porch and waited for my ride. My dad answered the phone, and I could feel the depressed energy in his voice. My father was the most energetic and positive individual the world has ever known, so hearing him like this made him nearly a stranger to me. I heard hesitation, fear, and solemn concern when he said softly, "Hi Steph." I can even recall responding slowly in a deep mocking tone, "Hi Dad... what's wrong?" He said, "Oh I am just worried about my appointment tomorrow." To which I replied, "What that you might be anemic? Oh my gosh, Dad, that's nothing — all you have to do is take some iron pills." He was confused. "Anemic? No, Steph, the doctor thinks I have cancer, and I'll know for sure tomorrow."

To be honest, the rest of the conversation is a fog. Afterward, he said words I never thought I'd hear from a member of my family. Words that only came out of the mouths of others, not Dad...not anyone from my family. My dad was healthy. He had never smoked a day in his life. He was active and young. It didn't make sense. The next twenty-four hours were a blur. I was glued to my phone, a hysterical mess; I was inconsolable but also couldn't stand the idea of being alone. I went to class as usual that Monday. I had a ceramic class in the afternoon, around the time we would be finding out. I went early, and told my professor about the call I would be receiving, and that it may require my immediate departure. The professor was wonderful and incredibly understanding. Sure enough, an hour in, I received a call from my mom. I can recall stepping out into the hallway. This class was held in a room at the end of a long vacant hallway in the art wing. I asked my mom what the doctor said, and I heard her voice begin to calmly slow and start to shake. I could virtually hear the tears welling up in her eyes and a ball of fear gather in her throat. I could tell she was trying to be strong for him and for me in her response. "Steph your dad is sick, but we need to be strong for him. The treatment is intense and very aggressive." I remember the feeling of my knees giving out after hearing those words. I immediately fell into a ball on the ground. I felt like the wind had been knocked out of me. I knew in that moment that my life would never be the same, but still, no one could have prepared me for the intense amount of growth that was about to occur over the next few years.

The doctors told my parents that with the rapidly progressive form of leukemia that he had, the majority of patients only live three months. Thankfully, my dad was not included in this statistic. Unfortunately, my father *was* incredibly sick for the remainder of his life, which was a total of nine years. When I arrived home again after that first week, my father had already gone through his first round of treatment. The strength of my mother brought my entire family so much comfort. Over the next nine years, my mom was by his side through hundreds of doctor's appointments, hospital visits, operations, surgeries, procedures, and so much more. Not only was she present, but she became so incredibly educated on his illness — and the different types of treatments, prescriptions, side effects and every detail of his illness — so much so that even the hospital staff, doctors, surgeons, and nurses thought my mother had a medical background as a result of her knowledge, engagement, and intelligent questions. She was so on top of things that at any given time she would know exactly what prescriptions he was taking and at what dosage. This is not only impressive because the list of scripts at any given time would be multiple pages long — and include so much detailed as to time to take, amount to take, circumstance to take, etc. — but also because his diagnosis was constantly changing as a result of infection, circumstance, etc. My mother knew more about my father's medical situation than any other person could possibly have had time to know. It brought him such incredible comfort for her to be present at visits and honestly she was invaluable, irreplaceable, because no one else could do what she did for him.

I told my dad I wanted to move home after he was diagnosed, and he told me no. He said, "If you come home I will feel like you have given up on me." Well, of course I would have never allowed him to think that — so I stayed at TCU with the agreement from my parents that I would be permitted to fly home every other weekend. I formed my class schedule so that I only had classes Tuesday through Thursday, which enabled my bi-monthly trips to last longer. From the time my dad began treatment that February to that May, his appearance transformed such that he looked like a completely different person. He had gone from an independent, towering man of 6'2, 195 lbs and a full head of hair, to a frail, 154-lbs bald man using a wheel chair. The transformation was devastating. Each week that I came home, my father looked more and more sick.

We were all a mess learning to cope and survive with our new reality. At this time, I was still so confident that I was my family's glue, that I could fix everything and everyone. I didn't realize, until I reflected years later, that I had frequent opportunity to escape this hell that my family was living when I was away at school, none of them could, this was their constant. I felt distance begin to build between my brother and me as time passed and I was away. I can recall calling home to tell my mom about an awesome grade I had just received. When she answered, she began to tell me about how awful everything was back home: details about my dad and my brother, on and on. We got off the phone without me ever having the opportunity to tell her about my great test score, in desperation of her approval. I decided to call my brother and help him out by giving him a heads up that Mom was having a bad day. When he answered, I said, "Hey dude, just a heads up Mom has had a really awful day so go easy on her." I thought for sure he would laugh and thank me for letting him know, but instead he said, "Steph, don't ever call me to tell me how Mom is doing. You are there and I am here." Then he hung up. My jaw has never hit the ground harder or stayed there longer. Thank God he said it, because I truly needed to hear those life-changing words as they offered me so much needed timely perspective. *No, Stephanie you aren't effectively running shit from Texas.* As time passed, my family unit was learning how to function without me, and it became more and more apparent every time I journeyed home.

I still traveled home frequently over the next three years, but I remember thinking, *Just finish college and then get home and fix everything.* My father was three years cancer-free, working on regaining his health and weight. I remember college graduation. My father was in the audience, along with my mom and brother. I was totally set after graduation. I had the supportive parents, the diploma, the ambitions and goals. I had *so many* ideas and goals. I remember thinking Life Coaching, Motivational Speaking, Writing a Book, and I knew my passion was to work with young women. I was told by the speakers I had interviewed as part of my position on Panhellenic, that I needed to write a book in order to gain speaking engagements. So I thought writing a book was my first step. I had no idea how to go about writing or where to start. I was terrified to begin that journey, so instead I decided to play it safe and make up a few excuses. I should add here that at the time, I totally thought these were actual honest reasons (not excuses) as to why I should put my dreams on hold.

Reflection:

Trust your gut...when something does not feel right, it probably isn't. I learned earlier than many, when someone is going through a hard time, it can be helpful to offer them a variety of suggestions of ways you can help them. Simply asking open-ended questions, like "What can I do to help?" will most likely leave you (and them) feeling helpless. In an instant, everything can change. Be as present as possible when you are with those you love, and soak up every possible minute.

QUESTIONS FOR REFLECTION:

- Can you recall a time in your life when everything seemed perfect, and then *wham*...life happened in an unexpected way?

- Have you ever thought you had more control over someone or a situation than you actually did? How did you come to the realization that it was out of your control?

- Have you ever had a moment where you felt your circumstances were unjust, e.g. *This doesn't happen to me or my family... this kind of stuff happens to others?*

* * *

NOTES

AFTER GRADUATION

During my senior year of college, one of my dearest friends was Hope, also from Saint Louis. The semester before graduating, she found out that the fashion department was not offering a class she needed to take to graduate until the following semester. This meant that she would not graduate until December, a semester after all our friends had graduated. The news was so upsetting that she was threatening to not finish at TCU. I remember thinking about how upset she was, and how this would have made me feel. Her mother had become ill and passed from cancer, right around the same time my father was diagnosed. I tried to put myself in her position. What would I want my friend to do if I was in her shoes? I thought about how I did not have a career taking me back to Saint Louis, and how I could write my book anywhere. At that same time, the family I had babysat for throughout college offered me a consistent after-school position to work with their children.

I decided to jump on the chance to stay in Texas for another six months. Hope and I searched for apartments with a six-month lease, and found nothing. We finally found the perfect apartment, however the lease was for a whole year. I signed the lease on the condition that she would help me find a roommate when the time came for her to move out, once she graduated. I decided to make my Texas stay a year-long venture.

The summer before we moved into our apartment, I decided to spend the summer with my family in Arizona.

The cancer had returned, and my father wanted to exhaust all options before going through chemo again. Treatment had been so intense the first time he experienced it that he was afraid he wouldn't survive a second time. So my mom found a center in Arizona that treats cancer from a holistic approach. My father agreed to try this first, and so off the family went to Arizona. I was confident that during the three months in Arizona I would be able to find a way to flood my father's body with vitamins and vegetables, for the first time in his life. I looked forward to strengthening my relationship with my brother, as the distance between our once close friendship was appearing to grow. Looking back on how terrifying being home for a weekend twice a month was, I truly cannot imagine living that way full-time, at my brother's age for as long as he did. So, having the summer off I decided the timing to fix my dad and become close with my brother was perfect. For me.

I was incredibly positive and optimistic about being able to help. I tried to get my father to eat, though he wasn't interested. Even more than lacking an appetite. he really wasn't interested in my constant nagging. I was so terrified of losing him — and I just remember thinking if he would just eat these vegetables and take these vitamins, I could fix this. I of course have no idea if that would have made any difference at all, but I wanted to believe.

Have you ever felt like you wanted something more for someone than they want it for themselves? Have you ever tried endlessly, put your life aside for that person, but ultimately weren't able to force him or her to do anything? If so, then you know that all you end up doing is beating yourself up more, because you feel like you are failing.

Meanwhile, the relationship with my brother was a whole other story. I've already explained how overprotective I have always been over Ryan. After all, he was my responsibility, or so I thought for basically our entire childhood, most of our teens, and into college. So, yeah, I am still working on it but I am so much better. Anyway, in Arizona, Ryan and I had rooms on a completely different side of the house than our parents. Our rooms shared a wall. We were also super close to the garage. I can remember staying up late just to make sure he was safely asleep, and instead in the middle of the night, often I would hear stirring. Many nights, I heard the humming of the car as he slowly backed out of the driveway. One night, I woke up around 4 a.m. and realized he wasn't home, a car was missing, and he wasn't answering my phone calls. Typical high school boy stuff I am sure — but he wasn't telling my anything. Before I left for college and my dad became ill, my brother and I use to tell each other everything. I became terrified, and had convinced myself that my brother was wrapped around a pole somewhere. "Oh my God how could I let this happen?" I thought. I remember crying, terrified that he would never come back, telling myself that the only thing I was supposed to do was take care of him — and I was failing. How would I ever forgive myself? Twenty minutes later, I was beyond coming unglued — so I decided to wake my parents, because obviously something awful had happened and I should absolutely wake them! *I probably should have woken them earlier*, I thought as I ran to their room.

I ran through the kitchen, down the hallway, and threw open the large wooden doors to their bedroom and shouted, "Mom, Dad!" Half asleep, Mom replies, "What is it, Stephanie? What's wrong?" I blurt out the whole story in between sobs. My dad chimed in, "Go back to sleep, Ryan is fine, he does this sometimes, he is fine." My tears dried immediately, but I remember walking away from their bedroom completely confused, and realizing that my family had a whole new kind of normal. They had learned how to function and get along together without me. Not only was I *not* the center, the glue, as I had thought, but they were living in a way I did not know where my place was any longer. Sad and defeated, I cried myself to sleep. The Ryan I had known didn't do this, why was this so normal for my parents? The dad I knew wanted to try to beat this, but obviously not the way I wanted him to beat this.

After about a week into my summer of fixing everyone, I was exhausted, defeated, and completely depressed. My mom found a counselor in the valley for me to talk to. I agreed, but not because I needed it, but because I thought my brother needed it — and I knew he would probably go if I went. My summer quickly turned into multiple counseling sessions a week, and not for my *brother* like I had thought. I needed to come to the realization that I could not control anyone but myself. I could not manipulate anyone I loved into saving themselves, or behaving the way

I thought they needed to be. This was a beyond painful realization. It also brought to light the fact that if I didn't stop trying to "mother" my brother, I would never have the opportunity to be his sister and our relationship would never be what I wanted — until I let go of trying to protect him and micromanage him.

The counselor suggested that we go to California and have brain scans done. These scans take images of your brain, and can detect exactly what is going on. They can display anxiety, depression, bipolar disorder, ADD, alcohol abuse, etc. These scans allow doctors the opportunity to properly diagnose and treat you, instead of making assumptions based on behavior, and risk prescribing a patient the wrong medication. *This is exactly what my brother needs, I thought. I will absolutely agree to this so that we can help him.* Mom, Ryan, and myself flew to California, and Ryan and I both had scans done. I couldn't wait to see the results with my brother. *Wait until he sees my perfect brain.* I doubt anyone will be surprised to hear that is not what the results showed. First, they showed us my results. The results concluded that I had anxiety, depression, ADD and a few areas of damage from college-era drinking. Up to this point in my life, I had never had a single prescription of any kind. I had known in grade school that I performed better on tests when in a private, quiet room, and with extended time. However, with the exception of extra time and tutors, I had learned to cope with the ADD stuff. Regardless, I couldn't even tell you what my brother's scans said. I didn't care at that point. I had just seen plain as day that the problem wasn't my family. My focus had been on fixing everyone else, but the evidence — the science — showed that I needed to help myself. I spent the rest of the summer trying a variety of prescription drugs and seeing my counselor and now psychiatrists. When you have ADD, anxiety, and depression, the result is some uppers, some downers, and a whole lot of crazy. Some drugs made me drop weight drastically, but also feel fucking spastic and crazy. I determined, after trying what felt like everything on the market, that ultimately I felt the best as my crazy self and not on crazy drugs. The side effects for me were far from worth it.

Reflection:

You cannot force anyone to do anything. The role of sister and mother are very different. Sometimes we think it is everyone else that needs saving but it is really ourselves.

QUESTIONS FOR REFLECTION:

- Have you ever wanted something more for someone than they wanted for themselves?

- Have you ever struggled with your most appropriate role in a relationship? Maybe this is a sibling you tried to parent, or a friend you tried to parent, or even a parent you tried to parent?

- Were you ever convinced the problem was with others' behavior, and then came to understand you were contributing to these dynamics more than you realized?

- Are there possibly problematic relationships in your current life that you could see from a different perspective?

* * *

NOTES

RUNNING AWAY

So after my wild summer, not accomplishing anything I set out to accomplish and learning a whole slew of information I was not expecting, I ventured back to Texas. I determined once I returned that instead of chasing my big scary dreams, my daily life would look like sleeping in, cooking food, watching TV, running some errands, picking the kids I worked with up from school, going home and making dinner, and doing it all again the next day. My boyfriend at the time lived forty-five minutes away, and I really only saw him on the weekends.

For the first half of the year, I stayed busy and had fun with Hope. Once her final semester was up and she graduated, I was left without a roommate, responsible for double my rent, lonely and miserable. I loved the family I was working with, so I started to take on more responsibility to be around them more often. I started assistant coaching one of the girls' basketball teams. I also began working out with a personal trainer regularly and he became a friend and confidant along my journey. In November, I visited home to support my dad and family as my father received a bone marrow transplant. I can remember sitting in the room as he lay in bed during the procedure: my brother and I on one side of his hospital bed, and my mother on the other holding his hand. It was peaceful, and our family was together. It was one of the easier procedures he went through, as it was as if a transfusion of blood was being given. At this point this procedure was my father's only chance of survival. I did not know at the time that only 24% of patients with my dad's diagnosis see their fifth year after being diagnosed. The transplant marked year four. After the transplant procedure, I traveled back home to Texas.

The six months that I lived alone were life-changing. I was miserable. I was incredibly lonely. I had zero girlfriends left in Fort Worth after all my classmates moved on, my boyfriend had just started his own company, and again, I lived far enough away that I rarely saw him. I was not any closer to my personal goals than I had been after graduation. I started to have a feeling that I was not where I was supposed to be at all. My savings were dwindling quickly as I was living far beyond my means.

I can recall one night as if it was yesterday. I was alone in my room and couldn't sleep. I began thinking about my grandmother and my book that I wanted to write. As I thought of Gram, instead of writing or starting my book, I had a better idea...a puppy. Yes, I should get a shih tzu puppy, bring him home and give him to Gram. She needs a dog — and I will totally train him before I go home. Brilliant idea. I stayed up the entire night researching shih tzu breeders in the area. As soon as eight in the morning hit, on a Saturday morning, might I add, I started making phone calls. Only one breeder had eight-week-old puppies left, and she lived about an hour away. She told me she could meet in an hour then, and with that I was off. As I pulled off the exit ramp and into the parking lot of the rundown gas station where we agreed to meet, I remember feeling excitement and anticipation come over me. Soon after I arrived, an old mini-van pulled in. A fairly large woman in an oversized yellow Tweety Bird sweatshirt stepped out of the car and opened the side of her van, motioning for me to come over. I walked over and introduced myself. She told me she had two males and a female puppy with her, and she opened a shoebox and all three were inside. I asked the difference between the males and females and she replied, "The males are nicer." I took her word for it, and looked in at the two males, the only difference I could see was in their colors. One was black with a white spot, and the other had many colors. The breeder referred to the one with different colors as "party colors," and with that he was mine. I handed her $300 cash, and just like that I was a mother. Well only for a while until Gram took him...so I thought.

I remember on the drive home, he was curled up on my shoulder. I already loved this little creature so much. He had been given the name Gizmo by the breeder, and I was determined to invent something more creative. I spent the next week researching names and calling him all types of things, but nothing stuck like "Gizmo" and so it was. Hope had moved out in December, and I was so lonely and broke by February that I decided a great idea was to get a dog? Hmm.

As March approached, I remember becoming angry. I was pissed at Hope for leaving me like this after all I had done for her. She hadn't moved out a lot of her belongings in her closet or her bathroom when she left after graduation, but she kept telling me she was coming back for them. By

March, I knew pretty confidently that I was going to be moving back to Saint Louis once my lease was up. Oddly enough, Hope had told a friend back home that she would be moving in with *her* upon her Saint Louis return — which wasn't appearing to be happening — and thus that friend called me to see if I knew anything about her plans. I knew if I moved home I didn't want to move back in with my parents, so Hope's friend Virginia suggested that since Hope wasn't moving in with her, that I should. It worked out well. I told Virginia I'd move in with her in May. In the meantime I was pissed. I was mad at Hope for leaving me and leaving all her stuff in a room I was paying rent for. I was mad at my boyfriend, who I partly blamed for my staying in Texas, for the fact that I was still here but he was working so hard that I never got to see him. I blamed my boss for not paying me enough so I was forced to leave. All of these people and external things were causing me unhappiness — of course I didn't have a hand in it at all…that's the way I saw things at the time.

I was the victim here, I hadn't had a hand in any of this! I can recall working out with my trainer, and telling him I was moving back home. He looked at me and said, "Just make sure you aren't running away from something here." I thought a lot about what he said, because it was jarring. Then I realized I wasn't running away from *anything* by leaving Texas, in fact I was finally putting an end to running away. I knew I needed to go home and help my family. I determined that if I lost my dad I would never forgive myself for hiding in Texas during his illness. Between March and

April, my mom told me to close my savings account back home, because the bank was closing. She informed me that I could use the funds to help me get on my feet as I move to Saint Louis.

There was quite a miscommunication between my mom and I as to which account, and just how much was in the account. There was a $10,000 difference in my checking and savings at that particular bank, and receiving that money made my twenty-three-year-old self think I was set. I moved home that May and had no rush to find a job as a result of my newly discovered wealth — and so I chilled. I spent the entire summer helping my parents when needed, waking up late, watching *Friends* episodes (I watched all ten seasons that summer), I started a softball league with my roommate, and we drank most every night. My new roommate Virginia worked, however she wasn't expected to report to her job until the afternoon. Most nights I was able to convince her to go to the bars. It was one crazy summer of drowning my savings and using the excuse "helping out my family" as to why I remained unemployed.

Believe it or not, when you are unemployed, young, and under the impression (however mistaken) that you are rich, money seems to go pretty quickly. By mid-August I was in a situation where I knew I had bills to pay...and my account was running low. I started looking for jobs as I was becoming desperate. I put together my first resume and scanned Craigslist every day for inquiries. I was searching for anything that would pay the bills. I was inquiring about nanny positions and teaching jobs. I heard back from a preschool that was hiring, a forty-minute drive from where I lived. I can recall driving out to my interview and knowing I did not have an ounce of experience or training that would be relevant for the position. During the interview, I spoke a lot about my experience as a nanny with children, and working in the inner city school as a high school student. I left the interview with no idea what to expect, and drove home. By the time I reached my roommate's bedroom to tell her all about the interview, the owner of the preschool was calling my phone to tell me I was the new teacher at her school. I was thrilled! *I had a job. I finally had something to really tell people when they asked what I was doing and I wouldn't go broke.* I should also mention that Gizmo was "too small" for Gram to take because of her eyesight deteriorating, and she feared not being able to care for him. The dog stayed with me, and I was glad.

Reflection:

Doing just enough to get by will NOT fulfill your big goals. Your goals will not come to you, you have to chase them. Learning for the first time that I didn't like being alone with me, instead of recognizing that as an opportunity to learn to love myself, I bought a puppy. I look back and realize it was so easy for me to blame all these other people for my unhappiness — but the truth was I was in that position because of choices only I had made.

QUESTIONS FOR REFLECTION:

- What do you like to do when you are alone?

- Have you ever thought others were the cause of your unhappiness, only to step back and realize if you had set better boundaries, or made different choices yourself, all your pain could have been avoided?

- Have you ever thought something like, *Well, I shouldn't have to tell him or her not to take advantage of me?*

- Have you ever made a purchase when you were lonely looking to find fulfillment?

* * *

NOTES

MY JOURNEY DOWN A
DEAD END ROAD

As the job started there were only eight students enrolled in the entire school — and the owner had a full staff. I remember the weeks of training, cleaning, and setting up for students. We were all making next to nothing, with limited hours, as we all rotated working with these eight kiddos. As time went on, with enrollment still low, the school began making staff cuts. I was one of the teachers to go. By then I had only worked a few short months with very limited pay and nothing to show for it. I remember being asked to leave, and getting in my car that day feeling defeated, lost, like an utter failure. I remember thinking how incredibly disappointed this news was going to make my parents, and drowning myself in a pool of shame.

I drove straight to my grandmother's house. I can see the memory of myself sitting on the ground next to her, sobbing, while she gently and methodically ran her fingers through my hair. She allowed me to weep and wallow for an appropriate amount of time before she stopped me. "Stephy," she said, "you never even wanted to be a preschool teacher." I stopped crying. She was right! This wasn't my dream, I didn't even enjoy it, it was incredibly inconvenient, and ultimately I was only doing it for money that it wasn't even making me.

Broke, unemployed, and back at square one, I remember taking a couple days as a breather while I contemplated the next step. That week at softball, the team went out to the bars after our game. It was there that I met a woman full of energy and life. We hit it off immediately, and ended the night singing "It's Raining Men" at a karaoke bar. Just after our performance, she offered me a part-time position. She had three children and a husband that traveled for work often. She hired me to pick up her kiddos, help with homework, cook dinner, and drive to after-school activities. In an effort to become closer to her middle child, I began volunteering to help her basketball coach with the team. I knew I wanted to coach young women, so I continued to network with women all over my city. I spent the fall meeting suggested women for coffee, and trying to get a feel for what organizations were offering empowerment programs for young girls.

I finally met an incredible psychologist who had put together a program for middle school girls, and was having a difficult time getting into the schools. We paired up and met with the principal of the school where the children of the family I was working for attended. Sure enough, our program was accepted and we began meeting with the girls once a week. I was feeling more on track to my true passion and was enjoying this work. I was then inspired to begin my life coach training. January 2011, I began a nine-month program to become a life coach. I completed my training alongside continuing to work with this family. At this time, I also began dabbling in photography. I started taking Christmas photographs for families and close friends.

That spring, my apartment flooded and I moved out of the place I was renting with Virginia — which meant moving home until I found a place. It was difficult to live back home for the first time since high school, for many reasons. I was not used to being constantly surrounded by the chaos that filled my family home. We constantly had nursing staff visiting my father, occupational therapists checking in, and at all hours of the day and night, I could hear my father yelling out in pain. There is no feeling more helpless than not being able to take pain away from someone you love and having to listen and watch as they experience it.

Once I graduated my life coach program, I stalled. I was technically ready to take clients — but that was terrifying. I didn't feel ready or prepared. I was extremely nervous to stop researching and studying and actually coach people. I continued to help the family I was working for, and decided I would offer coaching during the day. In the fall of that year, I was contacted by an old friend about a new business venture. It was a network marketing company that sold health and wellness products. I would not even consider making a business decision without my mom's help, so I asked my mom to come to a meeting and hear about the company. My mom researched the business plan and determined it was a lucrative compensation structure. I decided I could combine my coaching business and be a health and wellness coach. I worked on selling products and was off to a great start. I built a foundation and was selling quite a bit.

I spent the next few years doing a lot of small end jobs to pay the bills but was not any closer to my dreams. I told people when they asked what I did for a living that I kept my schedule flexible to help out with my father. From 2012 to 2014 my father lived more months in the hospital than outside of it. Following the bone marrow transplant, things started to change in his body. He would break out in horrible rashes, his skin was so incredibly fragile that you had to help him move in a specific way or his skin would tear off, and it was incredibly painful and required many bandages. Many people that were not accustomed to handling him made the mistake of helping him incorrectly, thus he was constantly covered in bandages. In the summer of 2012, my mother sold her company and I purchased a house. I spent months helping clean out her office and began accepting office supplies into my home. I filled the garage and basement with office furniture and supplies I thought I would sell or find uses for later.

Reflection:

Looking back it is so obvious that preschool teaching was a distraction. I also can't believe how much I relied on my mom's guidance to help me achieve success. I wish I had been able to see the excuses I was creating at the time so that I could have achieved my goals that much sooner.

QUESTIONS FOR REFLECTION:

- Have you ever been turned down, fired, rejected or derailed — and later realized it was a blessing?

- Name a time you let fear stand in the way of what you really wanted.

- Have you ever taken on a job or career that was not in alignment with your goals? What were some of the reasons you told yourself why? What were the real reasons?

* * *

NOTES

RESTORING FAITH
THROUGH LOSS

I lost my great-aunt and grandmother around the same time mom sold her office, and I accepted much of their furniture into my home as well. My grandmother and I were incredibly close. She was my father's mother, and the incredible woman I wrote of in my first book. From the time that she was admitted into the hospital until she passed away, many interesting situations occurred that restored my faith and spirituality.

Since my father's diagnosis I had begun to lose faith. I really struggled with why anyone would be subjected to so much torture. It also terrified me to think that he would fight for so long and never get to experience life the way he really wanted again. My father was violently ill in the other room of the same hospital Gram was sent to, and because of how contagious his illness was, anyone visiting him was required to wear masks, gowns, and gloves. My grandmother's condition did not seem to improve and she would soon be transferred to hospice. My father and grandmother wanted to see one another, but it was looking less and less like that would be possible. My father was in no condition to see anyone. My grandmother, for the first time ever, appeared to be encountering some confusion and it was difficult to hold a long conversation with her. In the short time the two were near one another, there was a window where dad's condition seemed to subside, and Gram's mind was vivid and clear as always. The nursing staff allowed my father to visit my grandmother during this window, and for a few hours the two visited and laughed. After their visit, my father returned to his bed where he continued to be ill for many weeks. His sickness came back many times before he was ever cleared of it, and he lived for months in hospitals until he would ever be released home. My grandmother was transferred to hospice.

The morning after she was transferred to hospice, Gram's state resembled a coma until she passed a week or so later. Every day I spent by her side, not knowing when she may decide to speak, or let go, and I wanted to be there. I happened to be editing a Christmas photo shoot near her bedside as she slept, and once I was finished I began to journal. I was listening as people would come visit her, I listened as they described how with her passing we would be losing her humor, captivating stories, and unique outlook on life. I became silently passionate about our responsibility, the responsibility of those who had come after her to carry on her legacy and positive perspective toward life. We each needed to learn from her and continue to spread the same life's joy she had displayed for us, to others. I journaled by her bedside for days. No one having a clue what I was doing, not even Gram. I left one night, knowing the end was near. It was dark and I was alone in my car. I can recall sitting at the stop sign just outside her complex and saying out loud, with tears welling up in my eyes and running down my cheeks, "I don't know if I believe in God, but I think I believe in angels, and Grandpa, I will know you are there to greet Gram on the other side if you let me hold her hand as she leaves the physical world."

I made a super risky deal with fate that night. I knew in my heart that if I wasn't holding her hand when she passed, that there was a good chance I would completely lose any ounce of faith I held onto. I also knew that if I was holding her hand, this silent deal I had just made had the potential to restore much of the belief that had diminished over the course of my father's illness. A few days later, my aunt asked for a few hours of my time to help clean out Gram's place, since Gram would not be moving from hospice. I felt guilty that Mom was occupied with Dad and was unable to help, so I agreed. We made a lot of progress, but the task took hours longer than anticipated.

Meanwhile, Mom was exhausted from weeks of hospital life, caring for Dad and staying by his side, and she didn't want to leave him but needed a break. I went to visit my dad, and then rushed over to see Gram that evening. When I entered the room, it was dark. Her breathing machine was out of her nose, she was gasping for air and sounded different to me than she had the day before. I flipped on a light, fixed her machine, offered her a sponge of water, and sat down near her. I hadn't heard her say a word in days. I yearned to hear her voice one last time. I knew my only hope was to get my father on the phone. I called him and said, "Hey Dad, Gram's not doing well and I think it would bring her comfort to hear your voice." I explained how that morning a lady had come in and washed her hair while she lay in bed. Some children stopped in, and delivered a fleece blanket they had made. I was trying to give him things to talk about. As I held the phone up on speaker, my father said, "Hey Mom! I heard you got your hair done today, do you have a hot date tonight?" She laughed. I saw her laugh. She had heard him and responded. Dad said, "Ok, well I am going to go, I love you, Mom." My grandmother replied, "I love you, too." That would be the last time my grandmother spoke or gave a response of any kind. I remember sitting there alone and holding her hand, just waiting. After a little time, my aunt, cousin, and mother arrived. The nursing staff came in to move my grandmother, and asked us to leave the room.

We sat in the hallways for what seemed like hours. About twenty minutes went by, and I was a panicky hot mess. I wasn't holding her hand, what if she let go? My cousin looked at me and said, "You know we lost her...right?" In utter disbelief, I didn't reply. They had to let me in. I had to be holding her hand. Finally, the doors opened and I rushed to her side, and saw she was still breathing. I grabbed her hand, and within minutes she took her last breath, while I was holding her hand. I drove away that night with a sense of relief and peace. Every other day I had sat by her side uninterrupted, but that day it had felt like a million things were pulling me in every direction. A million things were standing in my way, or perhaps making that moment of holding her hand even more magical, giving me a true gift.

Over the next few days, we tried to figure out every way possible to get my father released from the hospital so he could attend Gram's funeral. We stalled her services as long as possible in hopes that dad would be healthy enough to attend. In the meantime, I continued to journal in secret. I contemplated telling someone and maybe even asking to speak at her services, but continued to keep my writing to myself.

During one visit with my dad, he informed me that my uncle visited him and together they planned the funeral arrangements. He went through the layout on how the day would go. At one point he said, "The priest will speak, Uncle Terry will speak, and then you will speak." *Ummm...I will speak?* I stopped him. "I am speaking?" I mean, I had definitely considered speaking, but giving a eulogy isn't something that others usually just sign you up for. That's when Dad replied and said, "Yes, Uncle Terry said you wanted to speak." I paused in silence for a minute. *Had I completely blanked and told him I wanted to speak? No, of course not, I wasn't even sure I wanted to and offering to speak in front of all our friends and family that loved her so deeply is absolutely something I would recall doing.* After a long pause and much thought, I replied, "Oh ok."

My grandmother's was the first of three eulogies I would give in my mid-twenties. It's as if the universe said, "Well, you told me you wanted to do public speaking, but you aren't making any moves — so I will make some for you." My grandmother was making it very obvious to me that she was still around and watching over me. I felt like she had told my uncle, or had gotten it in his head somehow that I wanted to speak, so that the words I had written would be spoken. Weeks after her funeral, my mom and dad were eager to get her condo cleaned and on the market. I asked my mom what she would pay someone to clean Gram's place and determined that I wanted that money, so I offered to do the job. One sunny day, I ventured over to the condo to clean. All her personal belongings had been moved out of all her closets and cabinets. All that was left was furniture that they were using to stage for potential buyers. After cleaning the bathrooms, bedrooms, vacuuming, dusting, I went outside to blow the leaves off her porch. I was reaching down to unplug the leaf blower when I heard my grandmother say in my head, "Aw, sit down, honey — and have a drink." I thought, *Wow I have been here for too long, I am starting to make up scenarios in my head of things Gram would say.* But then it didn't really feel like that is what had occurred, so I thought, *Hey, before I leave I will just check her refrigerator and see if she would have had anything to offer me anyway.* I opened the left door and saw nothing but a box of baking soda, and then I opened the right and saw nothing but an airplane-size six-pack box of Sutter Home wine and two beers. I laughed to myself, and felt this wave of reassurance that Gram was indeed still with me.

It is crazy to think that loss and death restored my faith and belief in a higher power, but it's true. My dad remained ill and hospitalized for months following the death of my grandmother. It seemed as though he couldn't catch a break, and he became weaker and weaker. Finally, he was having more energy regularly and was able to come home. My brother moved in with me during all of this. I really believed that by removing him from the chaos and sadness that living at home presented, he would be more inclined to find a job and live a happier life. Over that year previously, my father had spent many more nights in the hospital than he had at home. After a million close calls and near-death scares, he was finally being released from the hospital. At that point he needed around-the-clock care, so my mom hired a nursing staff to assist him (and her) twelve hours a day.

Reflection:

It is so crazy to reflect on how desperately I wanted "stuff" to fill my happiness void. I am overcome with gratitude that I was able to restore my spirituality and connection to a higher power through the loss of my grandmother. I was able to experience such beautiful magic as a result of being present throughout the process of her spirit leaving earth.

QUESTIONS FOR REFLECTION:

- Have you ever experienced a defining moment that made you realize you were no longer a child?

- Have you ever tested or bargained with fate? How or when?

- Have you had an opportunity to find the beauty in loss?

* * *

NOTES

ANOTHER DETOUR JUST
FOR FUN

I had stopped working for that family and decided it was
time to spend time following my dreams. I began coaching
more clients, taking photography classes, and meanwhile
was still attending training for the network marketing
company. I received a call from one of my network marketing partners one day. She knew of a family in need and
thought I was the one who could help.

I was ready to shut this down altogether, as it sounded like
another nanny position — and I had closed that chapter
of my life, as it wasn't in alignment with my dreams. My
friend explained that the mother of this family was ter-
minally ill, and they just needed some support every now
and then. This hit so close to home, and I felt compelled
to help this sweet family. I knew my way around the cancer
center at the hospital, and I had been working with children for years — not to mention now I was a life coach
with much more knowledge to offer these young girls. I
knew there was no one else more equipped for this job and
then I wanted to help.

During my time with this family, my cousin, who had two
little boys of her own, was diagnosed with cancer, too. Her
time was very limited, as the cancer had spread throughout her body. Months of helping my cousin, my father, and
this other family took a serious toll on me. I started drinking and going out much more regularly. I was so incredibly
stressed, and seeing friends and partying seemed to be the

perfect distraction from the sadness and pain that was surrounding me.

I started a bowling league with girlfriends. It was an amazing excuse to see my friends and take my mind off everything in the middle of the week. The sadness and stress was really getting to me, and I was turning more and more to drinking as an escape. I had told a dear friend that I would accompany her to a fundraising trivia night with some of her coworkers. I offered to drive, since I didn't anticipate us needing a cab. After all, we were going to a charity work function. It was an ordinary night, and honestly, pretty low key since we were in the company of her much older coworkers.

We were having fun after leaving the trivia event and decided to go to a local bar. There was a band, and we were having fun dancing and meeting new people, as this was not a bar we frequented. The hours passed seamlessly, and before I knew it my friend was being picked up from the bar by the guy she was dating. I said goodbye to her, and went back in to grab my things and leave. Everything was there except my phone. I searched around in the dark room, but my phone was nowhere to be found. So frustrated, I left.

I got into my BMW loaner and drove away. Almost immediately, I saw a cop behind me. I was trying desperately not to make any mistakes or give the police officer a reason to pull me over, but it didn't matter. Soon enough, cue scene of the police officer and myself on the side of the road. As if I wasn't humiliated enough, a second police officer arrived.

I was taken into the station that evening and asked to call someone to pick me up. My phone was gone, and the only number I had memorized was my parents' house. I knew that would not be a call I would be making. I remember in that moment thinking that my parents were asleep, and there was no way I would call the house with my dad being ill and ask that my mother leave him to go get me, to bond me out of jail. This was my mistake and I was going to deal with it. My decision was spending the night in jail. A metal cot in the smallest room with a toilet in the center, cameras, and the brightest lights you've ever seen. It was beyond a bad night.

There, I was drowning in a pool of shame, terrified, and all alone. I wanted to blame my friend for leaving me after her function. I wanted to blame the individual that had stolen my phone. I wanted to blame the police officer for pulling me over for what seemed (at the time) like no good reason. It didn't matter who I blamed; the truth was a series of my decisions had brought me here and I was going to have to deal with the aftermath. I lay in the cell, awake for what seemed like days. Hours later, the police officer told me that there was someone in the lobby for me, a man, he said. I was terrified. Could it be that somehow my parents found out, and my ill father has made his way with my mother to get me? I would not leave until I knew exactly who had come for me. How could I ever face my parents? Their disappointment would be more than I could bear.

Thankfully, it was my boyfriend. He had known something was wrong when I didn't call him, and he was able to track me down. As we drove to get my loaner at the depot lot, I couldn't speak, I just cried. I was so embarrassed and ashamed. I was supposed to be helping others and making the most of my life — so what the fuck was I doing? The shame and disappointment I carried within myself was beyond words. The depot lot was not able to release the car to me until the dealership approved it. Of course, it was a loaner, and they had my actual car in their shop. I was mortified. Now everyone at the dealership would know what a huge fuckup I was. I would have to return there to exchange cars.

I found a lawyer and I will never forget our first meeting. I was ashamed, terrified, and holding back a river of tears. He asked me what my biggest fear was and I told him that my parents would find out. He laughed. "That's a first," he said. "Not that you won't be able to drive for a period of time? Not the thought of having a Breathalyzer in your car? Not hours of community service? Or thousands of dollars' worth of fees?" I'll admit none of those things sounded great, but they all still seemed better to me than worrying, troubling, or disappointing my parents.

I won't lie and say it was nothing, after all, my arrest meant spending the night in jail, months of community service, thousands in lawyer fees — and the vast amount of shame and disappointment I felt was awful. Before this event occurred, I will admit a part of me thought that I was invincible, a part me thought because I drove a BMW, and things like that only happened to others (and not me) — that I was someone above getting in trouble with the law... until I did.

After this life-changing event, I have become best friends with a few cab drivers, one in fact doubles as a playwright, and I have even gone to support him in his shows and even helped him sell tickets. On the rare occasion that my friends don't Uber or cab, I simply don't offer to drive or I offer and then simply don't drink. At all. Your mistakes only define you if you let them. I can recall my lawyer saying, "This one event does not make you a bad person. You have the power to repeat this mistake or allow it to make you an even better person than you were before." Then he said, "I hope you choose to be better because of this."

Two months later, in December of 2013, I lost my cousin and the mother of the family I was working with — days apart from one another. My father was at home and stronger than he had been months prior, and was thankfully able to attend my cousin's funeral. This would be the second eulogy I gave. Giving these eulogies helped me remember the importance of life, and living every day to the fullest. My cousin died too soon. She left behind two precious little boys. Her life helped to remind me that if I really wanted these dreams, I was going to have to stop making excuses and go after them. They weren't just going to come to me. Maybe that's why they call it "chasing your dreams."

I told my boss that I would be there to see him and his family on their feet and wait for him to find a more permanent solution for his family. I helped them through March, and then set out for a life coach conference in California to realign my dreams, life, and vision for the future.

Reflection:

I look back on this time of my life with such compassion. I was surrounded by cancer, death, loss, and illness in every area of my life. I see why I could get carried away when I was having fun with my friends. I wish at the time I had understood that it was ok to say "no" and take time for myself. Being pulled over after drinking was not an easy lesson to learn, however it did help me to slow down and really take a look at my life and how I was attempting to mask the pain and sadness I was experiencing.

QUESTIONS FOR REFLECTION:

- Have you ever gotten caught doing something and felt like you were drowning in self-reproach and shame?

- Have you ever made a mistake and tried to hide it from your parents, so not to disappoint them? Did you do a good job of handling it?

- How have you let a mistake from your past make you a better person moving forward?

* * *

NOTES

LOOK MOM NO HANDS...ALMOST

For me, I am most effective while on road trips. I am able to clear my head and brilliant ideas come to me. When I have the opportunity, I love to squeeze in a long road trip at least once a year. This conference in California seemed like the perfect excuse for a road trip. I flew to my parents' vacation home in Scottsdale, Arizona, and then drove to San Diego. The drive was the most fun I have ever had by myself. I drove a fun convertible, blared music, danced and sang the entire way. The drive itself was stunning. On the drive there are some flat grassy plains, then you drive through insane boulder mountains on the curviest of roads, eventually you approach massive sand dunes, as far as the eye can see. I adored this trip, and it was exactly what I needed to reset my business plan and get back on track. I can recall leaving this conference, energized, confident, and determined. I knew what I needed to do, write a book, do motivational speaking, work with young women — and nothing was going to stand in my way.

I got home from my trip, and received a phone call. A neighbor of one the families I had just stopped working for was in need. No, no, no. There was no chance in *hell* I would babysit for one more family. Except that in the case of this family, they already had a nanny — but the mother had just slipped and broken her ankle. The family needed a little additional help with their seven-week-old and only for a short period of time. Once her ankle healed, they would no longer need me. I liked the idea of the position expiring — and what were a few more months of postponing my dreams really going to do? I mean, the baby is going to sleep, and it will be good money while I organize for the next step. Ok, I will absolutely help out a few days a week. In March 2014, I began working for this family. A few weeks went by while the mother was lying around the house with her ankle in the air, and she began to hear interactions between her full-time nanny and the children as well as myself with the children. Ultimately she decided to let her nanny go... now what do you think came next?

Of course, by this time I had also fallen in love with this family. The mother had become my best friend, my confidant. The children were so sweet and adorable, younger than children I had worked with in years and they helped remind me of the true meaning of the word play. I had the most fun playing pretend, drawing with sidewalk chalk, and running through walls of bubbles...in tutus might I add (refer to StephGold_lifecoach on Instagram for video of this). If you don't want your son to wear a purple tutu don't allow a life coach to watch him...I am all about self-expression. I was in love with this family, so when their mother said, "It didn't work out with our past nanny and you do such an incredible job with our children. We love you, Steph, will you be our full-time nanny?" I of course said yes! I didn't think twice about my decision. I maintained a few coaching clients, families to photograph, the network marketing income, my parents hired me as a part-time employee to help with Dad, and the closing of Mom's business, all that filing and paperwork. I was not a step closer to any of my dreams, but I was happy enough that

I didn't realize it. As the baby grew and my duties evolved at the household, I began working less and less with the children. This family has very active little ones, involved in many after-school activities, thus I began helping out more with family chores.

So here we are. Yes, of course, you and I differ in age by a few years and maybe a few trainings, excuses, and years of stalling, but I suspect that where you are right now is about the same place I was November of 2014. I knew my goals, I was aware that I was not currently accomplishing them. But I was going to, someday. The difference between the Me in November of 2014 and the Me after college graduation in 2009 was that the me after graduation thought I had all the time in the world to accomplish my goals, and the me in the winter of 2014 realized I didn't. I should mention that at the time I was hands deep in tofu, frantically speed-reading the directions of the printout inside a beautifully compiled black and white cookbook, with a messy kitchen, dishes and measuring tools array. I was constantly looking at the clock and praying I had time to complete this task before the baby monitor signaled that in the blink of an eye I would be knee-deep in diapers and bottle making. This anxiety, in turn, causing it to become increasingly more difficult to perfect this quiche — and perfection wasn't even really a concern, it was just making sure whatever the end product was that it was edible and included all the ingredients that the recipe suggested.

Did I mention that all the while all of these concerns were flashing through my head there was also a dog at my feet, a dog that has been referred to as "food-motivated" and has been known to have a vertical jump that has proven capable of snatching and consuming an entire loaf of bread, sheet of brownies, large cheese pizza, and countless other food items from the counter before the individuals present are even aware an incident has occurred? No, this is not a German shepherd or mastiff, Bojangles is a puggle (pug beagle mix). Not a large dog, he is just wild and unpredictable enough to make this intense cooking experience truly an adrenaline-producing adventure.

Here is the beautiful thing. In this moment of epiphany for me, it wasn't about anything other than the fact that when I was truly present in that moment I realized this was a beautiful life. All of this chaos is something I genuinely look forward to having one day. My own crazy dog, my own babies crying from the monitor, knee-deep in my own insane cooking adventure (probably not the tofu part...but everything else). It was just one of those moments that you hear that wise voice inside you. Sometimes that voice is soft and sweet and sometimes that voice is as loud as a food processor turning a block of tofu into cream. The voice said, to me, quite literally, caps intended: "WHAT ARE YOU DOING? THIS ISNT WHAT YOU ARE SUPPOSED TO BE DOING! HOW DID YOU GET HERE, AND HOW IS HERE GOING TO GET YOU TO WHERE YOU NEED TO BE?"

So maybe you are most similar to the Me after college and you currently think you have all the time in the world to accomplish your goals. Maybe you'll spend your mid-twenties just as I did, focused in areas you have zero control, investing in friends that aren't investing in you, focused on helping everyone else but yourself, years in and out of essentially the same job with a different title and insignificant pay increases. Yes, maybe you'll be just like me and have way too much fun trying to consume happiness by indulging in unhealthy eating and drinking habits. Maybe you'll even start hoarding furniture in hopes that having more things will bring you happiness. Until one day you wake up at the end of your twenties, overweight, with a basement and garage full of shit you don't want, a social drinking problem, and essentially no closer to your dreams than you were four and half years prior.

Or maybe you'll be like Morgan working the job your parents respect, living in a beautiful condo, in the wrong relationship, and still fucking miserable. Or maybe you'll wake up like Pam, married to the wrong man, living in the wrong state, in a career that is not your calling — but one that everyone expects of you...you former valedictorian, you! Or maybe you are none of these women! Maybe you are like one of my other former clients and you stick it out and wake up in your forties with three kids upstairs, a husband you like some days, and somehow your dreams just never happened. Life happened instead, and a whole new set of excuses ensued.

Wherever you are in your journey, there is one thing I know for sure. You aren't where you want to be, you haven't achieved all your wildest dreams, because if you had you never would have opened this book. You wouldn't be searching for the answer, the keys to make this all smooth as butter. So, let's get to it! Let's establish exactly what you need to move forward. My hunch is that if you are reading this book you are ready to make strides to confirm you make the most of your twenties and execute your passion — so let's get started!

....

Reflection:

A conference or uplifting gathering can serve as the perfect battery charge for your goals and dreams. It is funny to reflect on how just when you think you are back on track the universe has a funny way of making you confirm it...are you sure you don't want another nanny job?...so here it is...you don't even have to do anything for it. I love the "Aha" moments that come when you least expect them... Hooray for tofu quiche!

....

QUESTIONS FOR REFLECTION:

- Name a time you had a blast and you were all alone. What were you doing?

- Describe a time you have had an epiphany or heard that voice inside you directing you.

- Have you ever made the same mistake twice or uncovered a pattern you find yourself stuck in?

NOTES

NOTES

CHAPTER 3

WHO ARE YOU (REALLY) AND WHAT DO YOU WANT?

Don't ask what the world needs. Ask what makes you come alive, and go do it. Because what the world needs is people who have come alive.

HOWARD THURMAN

After I left my job, and vowed to say goodbye to nanny-ing — or anything that resembled nannying, short or long term — for good, I called a publisher I had been in contact with over the years, you know, "before I was ready." The time was November of 2014, and I knew in order to achieve my dreams, things needed to change. I needed to change. I began to consider the different areas of my life, and areas that needed adjustment. I looked at countless balance circles, and ultimately created my own that I will go into depth about in the next chapter. I categorized the areas of my life, and then evaluated where I was spending my time. I then knew the areas that needed to be adjusted: some needed more attention to reach my goals, and some needed less. Ok, so, before I jump into the balance circle, let's lay down some of the foundation for you.

First, I needed to be reminded of what talents and gifts I possessed. I needed to know exactly how I wanted to be remembered, and the legacy I wanted to leave, and I had to develop a clear mission statement. Establishing your talents and gifts maybe something that comes to you naturally. For me, an assessment called "Strengths Quest" allowed me to verbalize my gifts in a way that was empowering, and made these clearer than ever before. If you can easily list five strengths, then do so below. If you are more like myself and struggle to verbalize them, I suggest purchasing the book *Strengths Quest* and taking the assessment included in the book purchase. If that does not seem feasible or like the right answer for you, but you are still struggling to verbalize your gifts and talents, I highly recommend considering the activities you participate in where you find yourself losing track of time. For me, I lose track of time while writing. I also love to socialize and connect with people. And not surprisingly, my top strength is Communication.

If you are still having a hard time thinking of five, another thing to consider is what were you *picked on* for as a kid? People always told me I told too many stories and talked too much. No surprise, given that my top strength is Communication. In Strengths Quest, Communication is described as follows: "You like to explain, describe, to host, to speak in public, and to write...you feel the need to bring events to life, to energize them, to make them exciting and vivid."

We all want to become clear on our purpose...our big assignment from the Universe...and for some people that is super clear and obvious and for others we receive sign after sign that we gather along our journey until the whole picture comes together and our destiny is crystal clear.

What are three things you are excellent at? Know that these also may be the things that have stood out to people over time, and kids would make fun of you for: "you talk too much," "you have a story for everything," or for someone else it may have been, "you are a nerd." Justin Timberlake said while on *The Ellen DeGeneres Show*, "I grew up in Tennessee, and if you didn't play football, you were a sissy. I got slurs all the time because I was in music and art...I was an outcast in a lot of ways...but everything that you get picked on for, or you feel makes you weird, is essentially what's going to make you sexy as an adult." So one way of coming up with things you rock at may be thinking about qualities or hobbies you were picked on for having.

Yet another way to come up with your gifts and talents may be to consider hobbies or activities you do that cause you to lose track of time. You may be working on a project and you look up and four hours have floated by. What activities are you doing when that occurs?

Identify five of your strengths, gifts, and talents below.

1.

2.

3.

4.

5.

Now that we know what comes naturally for us it is essential that we establish how we wish to be remembered. There is an exercise I find most helpful when sorting this out. I will walk you through it right now but I find the most helpful way to do this exercise is through listening. You can find a recording of this guided meditation paired with a journal exercise by clicking on the link on my Instagram page or by visiting www.StephGoldLifeCoach.com and clicking on the box marked "Dreamers."

Meditation and journal exercise

I highly suggest reading this in a dark room by candlelight. Sitting on the ground or lying is fine. You will need a pen and paper, and I urge you to have both of those items close before you begin. I also encourage you to do this exercise when you are comfortable and alone.

First, close your eyes and take four cleansing breaths. Let go of all tasks on your "to-do" list or any tension or stress in your day. Breathe in, a four count, hold for a four count, and release on a four count. Repeat this breathing three times while you clear your mind. Now I want you to imagine you are at a funeral. You recognize everyone in attendance. You see friends from all ages and years of your life. All of your family is present. Old teachers and professors, coaches and mentors you've had are present.

You are not sure who this funeral is for, but you stand in line to pay your respects. As you come closer to the open casket, you peer in and see yourself. You sit down as you listen to each individual stand up and say how you impacted his or her life. Your closest friends and family are describing the impact you made on the world and how the world is a much better place because of you. You have inspired family and friends beyond your wildest dreams. Now, I want you to set the timer on your phone for three minutes. I want you to start writing, specifically, everything these individuals said about you. How exactly did you impact the world? What specific things did you do to change and inspire the lives of others?

MEDITATION AND
JOURNAL EXERCISE

When the alarm goes off, stop writing. Then, I want you to look over the words you wrote or have bullet-pointed down, and answer these questions:

- How will your life change the world?

- How do you want to be remembered?

Now we are going to take your responses to these questions and form your mission statement.

My mission statement reads:

To positively impact the lives of Millions of women world-wide. To help guide women to a life filled with freedom, fulfillment, joy, and purpose. To aid women in the discovery of their best life now, and to support them in the achievement of their wildest dreams.

I have had this mission statement since I was in college. But simply establishing my strengths, discovering precisely how I wanted to be remembered, and knowing my mission statement was not enough. I had discovered those three key components in college — so why, five and a half years later, was I still working for a family as a babysitter? *Excuses.* Lots of intricate and gorgeous pre-packaged excuses that I referred to as "reasons" or momentary obstacles that were holding me back. I saw myself as super young, with plenty of time to chase my dreams, and the truth is that fear of failure and lack of direction were the main forces holding me back.

I am about to tell you about the moment every great excuse I had been holding onto was ripped from me, but before I do, I will first tell you that I have always had a million ideas of ways I could make my print on the world. Motivational speaking, counseling, write a book, start a summer camp, life coaching...and I would obsess over the amazing possibility of one of these ideas and then a few months later have a new brilliant idea and change my mind.

The reason I spent the majority of my twenties failing at everything wasn't because I wasn't capable — it was simply *the fear* that I wasn't capable, that I would let down the only individuals I cared the most about, the ones that had given me everything, my family. How did I cope with that fear? I became a professional at buying and selling excuses. I invented the most brilliant and intricate excuses, so fabulous in fact that not only did I believe them to my very core, but I was able to convince nearly everyone I encountered of them. I was able to effectively postpone the first five years after I graduated. I did this by keeping myself small, playing life safe, and buying and selling a ton of excuses.

I had finally determined, by leaving the family I had been working with, that now was my time. My dad was stable. He was out of the crazy rollercoaster hospital cycle he had been in the two years before. He was living at home, and had good days and bad days. At this point, however, even his good days consisted of spending hours getting ready (which nearly exhausted him) and maybe getting out for a drive or fun activity for a few hours with a member of our family, one of his friends, or one of his nurses. His best days were still not what anyone would ever hope for on their worst day, however the fear of losing him at any moment, like I had while he was living in and out of intensive care, had subsided. With the help of his nurses, my family needed my help much less, and I was able to spend the time I had with my father visiting with him, watching funny shows, communicating — rather than spending that time with him caring for him, which was a blessing. I felt like now was the time to write.

I was also asked by a friend to photograph her wedding in Mexico. I was beginning to make all these exciting shifts around my twenty-eighth birthday, which was November 2014. I determined that I would spend my twenty-eighth year trying new things and taking risks. I began saying "yes" to adventure and putting myself out there. I agreed to photograph my friends' wedding in January. Then, I decided to begin writing my book in Arizona the week after the wedding. I set out for Arizona with my dog, thinking I would be gone a few weeks, in an incredibly inspiring environment, essentially alone and would receive the clarity and stillness I yearned for with the birth of my book. I left on a Wednesday, then on Saturday evening my mom arrived. On Sunday evening, my mom received a call...it was my father's doctor. The day my mom left for Arizona, my father began to have severe stomach pain, and had been rushed to the hospital. The doctor instructed us to come home immediately.

My dad's illness had presented hundreds of fake-outs over the nine years he was ill. Even though this sounded serious, I was in disbelief that it actually was. I had seen my dad, I had spoken to him on the phone Friday night. *He was fine.* I looked at my mom and asked, "Should I really book a flight and come home now, or should I wait a day until you assess the situation?" She looked at me and said, "I think you should come home now." I still didn't believe it was serious. Why would I? He was so much better than a couple years before. There was no way the end was now. So I reluctantly boarded a flight home. When I arrived at the hospital, my dad was in intensive care. He was in so much pain that the doctors had him on a morphine drip that was causing him to sleep most hours. A few days passed with countless doctors, surgeons, and hospital staff members evaluating my father's condition and offering suggestions. My mom was left to have these discussions with his team of doctors because my father was essentially in a medically induced coma to manage his pain.

All options were exhausted. The next week of my life was one huge fucking nightmare. His condition was beginning to sink in. Slowly, as the days were passing, I was beginning to realize this might actually be the end. He might not recover this time. As quickly as I would think it, I would try to replace that horrible thought with positivity. As the days passed with no improvement, my hope became less and less. Once he was not receiving any further treatments, it was clear. Watching someone you love suffer is the single worst thing one could ever witness — and of that I am confident.

The next few days were a depressing blur. The last time I heard my dad speak was when my brother arrived, and he was so thrilled that he perked up and said, "Hi boy!" I can recall the last days vividly. They were so completely different than I had ever pictured.

I always thought the end would present us with great conversations or words of enlightenment and encouragement. My dad was my hero, he was the most positive individual I have ever met. He loved music, adventure, travel, old cars, tradition, celebrations, and family and friends dearly. The night my father passed, I knew my life would never be the same. That night, I not only lost my father, #1 life cheerleader, biggest supporter, travel partner, adventure seeker in my life who always found a way to push me and cheer me up, the most positive person I had ever met — I also lost what I had made into my greatest excuse not to <u>chase</u> my dreams. I didn't know it in that moment, but I soon realized that all these great, legitimate "reasons" I was not chasing my dreams were not actually *reasons* but *excuses* — and it became piercingly evident.

Not only was I telling myself I needed to help my father, but I had also been saying I needed to help my brother and mother as well. When my dad passed, I still carried the thought that I needed to help my mother and brother. Now, my time would be occupied by cleaning out the house I grew up in, selling it, helping my brother find a new place to live, and helping him move in. I also determined that my father's life deserved a celebration in his honor that was up to his standards and caliber. I immediately called my publisher and told her that there was no way I could write my book *right now*. I had far too many arrangements to make, and I was so depressed with the loss of him, that there was no way I would be able to write a book about happiness during the most difficult time in my life. She understood, and told me to call her back when I was ready.

A few short weeks went by before I realized if this book I had been talking about since college was ever going to be written, the only time *was* now! With the loss of my father, my family began to receive countless emails, letters, cards, and messages of people describing how much his life had touched, inspired, and impacted theirs. I knew that if I didn't write the book about my grandmother's example for life, it would quickly become an entirely different book. I called my editor back, and told her I was ready. I began writing, alongside planning my father's celebration of life, which actually contained more details and planning than one would think. The planning resembled more of an event, on the order of a wedding reception. I began writing in March to publish in May — a few days after my father's party.

In 2015, every excuse I had been carrying was ripped from me and completely exposed. I had always looked at my father's illness as a "reason" not to chase my dreams but in actuality it was simply a really great excuse. Now that I have written my first book, I can look back and realize that I totally could have been writing alongside my father's illness. He would have been devastated to know that I was using his sickness as an excuse not to follow my dreams. All he ever wanted was for me to soar and excel in my passion and purpose. Once my excuses were identified, there was no turning back — I was forced into action. I was forced into my life's work and passion. I was forced into my freedom and happiness.

Isn't that fascinating? Because once you've seen the truth, the light, you can't "unsee" it. Now that I had identified my excuses, I couldn't use any of them any longer to hold me back or stunt my growth. And here is the even crazier part: once I saw what an excuse could look like, or how it could show up, I began to recognize new excuses even sooner, before I took them on and started to believe them. I will share with you some of the excuses I believed for *years* in my twenties, and then I want you to start writing some of yours down.

After I graduated, an excuse I became *obsessed* with was the thought: "I need to lose weight." I went to countless doctors, personal trainers, coaches, and all other gurus to find the answer to my weight gain. What I found, after years of little to no progress, was that if you ask someone who solves problems to give you a reason for your problem, they will. It doesn't necessarily mean it's true, or that their solution will be effective for you. I would think "How can I be a life coach if I can't lose weight?" The answer I would come up with was, of course, "I can't," so instead of working on my coaching business (because that was big and scary) I will spend my energy and focus on weight loss instead. And it's no wonder I wasn't losing the weight, because holding onto the weight was the one thing keeping me from having to do the *scary* thing (which was working on my business).

What I have found through my personal experience and with clients too, is that one excuse is not enough security — so we begin inventing all kinds of new excuses. *I need to clean my house.* I learned a tool in my life coach training called the "living space tool" which essentially looks at your living space as a metaphor for what is going on inside of you personally. I knew that it would be hypocritical to coach individuals in this way, so subconsciously I began filling my house with loads and loads of stuff. My grandmother died, and I took a ton of her furniture. My mom sold her office, and I took carloads of office supplies, computers, and furniture to my house. My great-aunt died, and a ton of trinkets and furniture that meant nothing to me came home with me anyway. Soon I had successfully filled my garage, basement, and closets in my house with a ton of shit I didn't want, need, or care about. This of course resulted in the excuse, "I need to clean and organize my house."

Some excuses will be small and easy to spot, like for instance my excuse, "I am so young." When I first graduated, I was in my early twenties and I did live as though I had all the time in the world to accomplish my dreams of having a speaking career, a book, and becoming a life coach. Then, in January of 2011, just a year and a half after graduating college, I began my nine-month intensive life coach training course. It didn't help that the vast majority of my peers in the training were at least twenty years my senior. All that did was fuel my belief that I had all the time in the world, because "I was so young." Well, guess what happens when you sit around for years believing that excuse? You wake up one morning and you aren't so young anymore — and you still have yet to achieve your goals.

The "I need to help my dad" excuse also translated to "I need to help my mom" and "I need to help my brother," so if you are still thinking *you* have any impact on the progression or success of anyone else's life — and that your life and happiness means less than their happiness and well-being, so you'll just put yourself aside for now — write that excuse down first, because that is going to be a big fat "oh no you don't" from me. I'd also like you to consider that (potentially the most effective way) you can help others in your family, or close friend group, is to succeed for yourself. This way you will inspire them to do the same, or you may empower them to begin to help themselves.

Some excuses are disguised as deep-seated beliefs that we have carried with us for years and years. In third grade, I was struggling to learn how to read. I remember having days' worth of tests performed on me as a child, to determine what specific "learning disability" I had. My mother was so concerned with my well-being, and wanted to provide me with the best education and necessary attention possible. I spent years attending sessions with after-school tutors and in learning centers on the weekends to help raise my tests scores, while in school I had testing accommodations. I can recall exactly how it felt when the resource teacher would come to the classroom door and call out my name. That meant it was time to leave my class and receive extra help in another room, separate from my peers. I can picture my teacher walking around the room, handing out tests, and when I was handed mine I had to leave the room, because I received extra time as part of my accommodations for my learning diagnosis.

As a child I didn't understand what is happening. Why am I different? Why didn't I score as high as other students when sitting in the classroom taking a test, as they each did. I can recall kids teasing and saying, "Why does she get to go? That's not fair." Lacking the knowledge or understanding to explain it to them, or understand it myself, I struggled.

At the first high school I attended, I was scoring terribly low in Spanish class. After a few months of tutoring and accommodations when testing, the school exempted me from taking a foreign language — and said that as a result of my learning disability I would never be able to learn a foreign language. When I transferred schools, the high school I graduated from had an entirely different classroom approach than the previous school, and I excelled. Not only did I take a foreign language, and pass with flying colors, but I also made the Dean's List my senior year and had the best grades of my life. It was not the fact that I graduated from a less difficult school than the two schools I had attended previously. Trust me, plenty of my high-school peers went on to attend private universities and many even Ivy League schools.

Even though my senior year grades were enough to support the belief that I was intelligent, it was too late. I had spent my whole life thinking I was inferior and less capable than my peers intellectually. So, why wasn't I writing a book? "I wasn't smart enough." That excuse was much less obvious for me to find, because I never told anyone I felt that way. It was just something I believed, deep within me, and perhaps even forgotten to myself. There may be a limiting belief you are holding onto that is a very polished, long-believed concept that holds you back. One which is ultimately a big fat ugly excuse polished as a "very good reason."

Ok, so now that you've heard a few of the awesome excuses I held onto and bought and sold to others for years — it's your turn. Below, I want you to write down five good reasons to keep you from pursuing a goal or achieving your highest potential right now. What is holding you back? Identify your excuses below.

Ex. *I need to help_____ (dad, mom, brother)*

I need to lose weight

I need to clean my house

I am so young

I am not smart enough (some old lies we have carried with us)

Your excuses

1.

2.

3.

4.

5.

If you are someone whose matrix of excuses has just imploded, I have great news for you! The truth is once we are able to recognize one of our excuses, many others can become revealed as well. It can be incredibly overwhelming to have all of your excuses collapse on you at one time, however the great news is releasing your excuses in this way is essential in accomplishing your dreams. So if this sounds like you, the fabulous news is you are so much closer to bliss — hang tight!

You have identified your strengths, and you are now super clear on how you want to be remembered and the legacy you want to leave. We have verbalized it into a mission statement, while you have learned those three things are not enough, and so we have established your core excuses that will show up and stand in your way.

Now it's go time. It is time to become super selfish so that you can serve others. If you are anything like myself (and most of my clients), selfish is hard. Selfish is really really fucking crazy hard. So let's dive into the balance circle.

NOTES

NOTES

NOTES

CHAPTER 4

TAKING CARE OF YOU SO YOU CAN TAKE CARE OF OTHERS

If you want to awaken all of humanity, then awaken all of yourself. If you want to eliminate the suffering in the world, then eliminate all that is dark and negative in yourself. Truly, the greatest gift you have to give is that of your own self-transformation.

LAO TZU

After my father died, many excuses to not accomplish my goals were ripped from me. People whose time I honored more than my own were taken from me, and I was forced to look at myself and consider what I really wanted out of life. After my father passed away, my most logical excuse would have been to say I needed to be there for my brother and mother. That was not an option, however, my brother and I deal with difficult situations differently. While I run to loved ones to be consoled during hard times, my brother prefers to be alone. This, of course, would make it difficult to try and "take care of him" if you will.

A few weeks after my father passed, my brother moved out. My mother immediately began traveling. It was the first time in years that she felt comfortable leaving town, because she did not have my father's health to worry about. In the past, even under the care of nursing staff and the help of my brother and myself, my father almost always took a negative turn medically when my mother left town. I can't really explain the cause: maybe it was coincidence, if you believe in that sort of thing, or maybe it was mental. Either way, mom rarely left town without my father being sent to the hospital after her departure.

Without my brother and my mom to have to take care of, I was running out of excuses. I began to consider actually using a tool I learned to use with clients, to help me figure where to focus my own time and energy. This tool is referred to as the Balance Circle. There are countless options for these circles. Some contain many categories and some much less. When searching to find the perfect one to use, I was at a loss. None of them seemed quite right for me — so I created my own.

Relationships

Growth

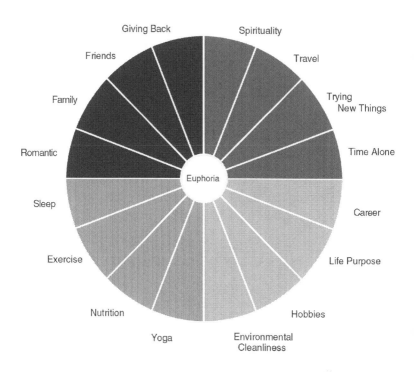

Giving Back

Spirituality

Friends

Travel

Family

Trying
New Things

Romantic

Time Alone

Sleep

Euphoria

Career

Exercise

Life Purpose

Nutrition

Hobbies

Yoga

Environmental
Cleanliness

Health

Productivity

My goal was to get back into alignment with my goals, and to make sure I was putting in the energy in areas of my life that needed it. I had a reason for creating my own balance circle. I felt many circles I came across had been missing key areas that I felt were important to help me live the happiest life possible. I will explain why each category is essential.

RELATIONSHIPS

You'll notice the majority of the balance circle is about *you*. That is not by mistake. For my clients and myself, it is incredibly easy to put ourselves last and focus more on how we can help others. The truth is we can't help others until we help ourselves. With that being said, we are social beings and it is important to spend time honoring the relationships in our life that are important to us.

You will notice under the umbrella of relationships there are four categories: Romantic, Family, Friends, and Giving Back. Although these will fluctuate from day to day, the important thing to consider is that generally (and overall) we do not thrive when we are completely neglecting one area or giving a couple of areas too great a share of our attention. I know this was extremely important for me to learn, as there were times in my twenties I was neglecting my family in an attempt to protect myself from my father's illness, like during the year I spent in Texas after college. Then again, there were also times it was easy to occupy my entire week with social events with friends, and completely neglect the other relationships in my life that were equally as important — including the relationship with myself.

In the past, I have spent far too much time trying to please my family, friends, and significant other. I would drop things I wanted to do, rearrange my schedule for others without a thought, even at the drop of hat. There were times my mom would call and needed something, and suddenly I was off doing it and had left behind all else.

Just yesterday I received a text from my mom reminding me that I owed her a car wash. The backstory is that a couple weeks ago, my mom was out of town and I borrowed her SUV so that I could navigate the snow that was coming in. I returned her car just before leaving for the airport, and did not have time to wash it. I told her that when I returned I would take it for a wash. I have now been home a week and got busy with my own deadlines — and I completely forgot to wash her car. She texted me asking about the wash. The "old me" would have immediately stopped writing my book, which was on my schedule all day yesterday, put my plans to write on pause, and immediately run over there to get her car and get a wash. After all, I do owe her one and I did say I was going to. The difference is that today I understand something I did not back then. She will not value what I do not value. If I stand up and walk out, pushing aside my writing, she will not value my writing time — because I will show her that I do not. So here is what I said: "Oops! Totally slipped my mind. I have a huge deadline for my book due tomorrow, but I can take it on Thursday." Her response: "I thought it was supposed to already be handled." She was pushing back. She was right, but the mistake already happened. I needed to find the win-win that was still possible. So I wrote back: "It totally was, I'm sorry, completely slipped my mind. I will get to it Thursday."

Understand that if you have been pushing things aside for the relationships in your life for a long time, it is normal to expect some pushback. My mom didn't respond, "Hey, awesome! See you Thursday." But instead with more expectance of immediate compliance...get to it like you said you would. This is where beginning to put up new boundaries and expectations will be key (and life-changing) for you and your relationships. Remember you teach people how to treat you. If you do not value your time or schedule, neither will anyone else.

Another example of this can be seen in romantic relationships. I can recall numerous times I told myself I was going to make it to yoga, or to the gym, and then my significant other would call — after work, you know, wanting to do dinner. I would drop whatever I had planned to make him happy. This behavior replicated into my friendships as well. Soon the end result was a bunch of people who began to expect me to drop everything for them. Their attitudes, and clear lack of respect for my schedule, would anger me beyond reason. I finally concluded that people didn't respect my time or my job — because I was teaching them not to. I was not showing my schedule or plans respect by continually dropping them for the needs or desires of everyone else.

Remember my old roommate, Hope? The one I was so mad at — and ultimately ended friendship with — because she never found someone to fill her room, and instead made it my responsibility to dispose of all the stuff she had left in my apartment after she moved out? Well, here is how boundaries would have shifted that entire situation. If I had really meant for her to find a roommate before moving out, I should have asked her to put it in our contract. I also could have said, if in the case you are not completely moved out by (fill in) date, you will be required to continue to pay your half of the rent. I did not truly set any boundaries for myself, and ended up doing a lot of finger-pointing, when the truth was that my lack of boundaries was just as much a contributor to the continuation of the situation as her behavior had contributed by creating it.

If you find yourself in a similar situation, I cannot stress the importance of boundaries with family, friends, and romantic relationships enough. Relationships and connection to other human beings are essential for our happiness. Happiness chemicals are released in our brains when we hug those we love, are in the company of our friends, and when we spend our time helping others. However, it is essential that we remember that while the relationships in your life are incredibly important, they are just a fraction of the entire puzzle. To paraphrase a little Simon Sinek, no matter how much you love those individuals, you cannot serve them until your serve yourself.

Giving back is an area of relationship that is crucial to our happiness. The summer before I began my freshman year, TCU offered the students different camp options to give the incoming students an opportunity to get to know some of their peers before school started. There were a few options. One involved a tour of Fort Worth, the city our campus was located in, another camp involved adventure and going out into the wilderness, and yet another involved volunteering. I don't recall much about this camp or what exactly we spent our time doing, however I do recall one thing. At the end of camp, we were all gathering in an auditorium to reflect on our experience. A few of the counselors were asking our group what some of our takeaways were from camp. One counselor asked the group, "Why did you choose this camp over the others?" One of the students in my group answered, "I chose this camp because I wanted to be friends with other people who enjoyed giving back — and I wanted those people to be the first I met at TCU."

His response resonated deep within me. It was my truth. He articulated exactly how I felt but had been unable to verbalize. Giving back, the kind I am talking about, goes beyond donating clothes or furniture. As important as that is, the kind of giving back I am referring to involves your time and talent. Giving back also involves human inter-action. While donating your time to the board of a non-profit is a form of giving back, the type of giving back I am referring to involves human interaction with those in need, making your service more personal and direct. I include this type of giving back in my retreats because there is something magical that happens with human interaction in the form of physically aiding someone in need. "This is how you get oxytocin (one of the four brain chemicals — neurotransmitters — that produces happiness): doing nice things for people that require you to sacrifice a little bit of time, a little bit of energy, something you will never get back," says Simon Sinek in a talk about *Why Leaders Eat Last*. Here is the super cool thing about oxytocin: when you give to someone you get a shot of happiness, the person you did the nice thing for also gets a shot of oxytocin, and anyone else who witnesses the act does as well. Providing that much happiness, and multiplying happiness, is one of the major reasons I choose to arrange for my clients to give back in this way.

GROWTH

This is my favorite portion of the circle. Growth consists of Traveling, Trying New Things, Spirituality, and Time Alone. I love growing and pushing myself out of my comfort zone! Traveling is also a key component of growth. Seeing new sights, witnessing the way other cultures live, can be life-changing and incredibly powerful. Growing up with my father in the travel industry enabled me to see so many unique places and experience so many different cultures. I decided to live on a cruise ship for my study abroad program. I traveled to eight countries in seventy-three days. It was the most eye-opening and life-changing summer I have ever experienced. I traveled to Norway and witnessed extreme sports week. I saw Saint Petersburg, Russia, I toured the Nile River, and saw the pyramids in Egypt. It was truly the most life-changing experience to witness so many different cultures, see different lifestyles, hear so many different languages, and to experience for a brief time another culture's way of life.

Making an effort to try new things is an essential component of growth. It is so easy to fall into mindless habits in everyday life. I found myself, at the age of twenty-seven, rarely trying new things. I bought the same items at every trip to the grocery store. I was participating in the same hobbies, activities, sports, TV shows, etc. I became aware that I was rarely trying something new or putting myself out there. I decided with the arrival of my twenty-eighth birthday that I would make it a point to try new things. I kicked off my year of trying new things with a painting birthday party! My closest friends and I took a painting and wine class, and had a blast.

From there, I began making an effort to try new things and to visit the vast world of unknown. That January, I traveled to Mexico to photograph my friends' wedding and decided to take a half-day excursion by myself. I traveled with a guide into the Mayan jungle. When I arrived just outside the jungle, I hopped into a large off-road vehicle. After about a fifteen-minute ride, I went zip lining over the Mayan jungle. I rappelled into the Cenote, which are underground freshwater river patches. I was then blessed by a shaman in a cave, went hiking through the jungle, and stopped at an authentic Mayan village for the most incredible meal. After my visit in the village, I went snorkeling and saw all these underwater cave formations. It was the most incredible trip, and I cannot express how amazing it was to try something like this for the first time. I never would have found this place, or tried this experience, if I hadn't made a point to research and look for something to try before my arrival. I set out to try new things, and made it a point to do so. I also set a goal of adding something new to my grocery cart each week. When I was out to dinner, I would order a dish I had never had before. It is amazing the amount of things you will learn about yourself once you begin taking steps to venture outside your comfort zone.

Spirituality is an area of growth in my life that continues to strengthen. There are ways to nurture your spirituality through meditation and prayer. I find it easiest to write letters to my deceased father as my form of prayer. I have experienced so much death of loved ones in my twenties, and I have found that paying close attention to visitations in my dreams and other spiritual encounters has aided my continued belief in a power greater than my own, and in the belief that there is a bigger picture and energetic connectedness among all life. I described in depth my experience with the passing of my grandmother, and how that prompted a spiritual awakening for me.

Time alone is essential for growth. When you think about the time you spend alone I want you to consider the time you spend away from electronic devices or noise of any kind. If you are someone who practices meditation without the help of electronics, it can be considered alone time. However, if you are like me and prefer guided meditation, I would categorize that as building your spirituality. Journaling is an incredible option to do during your allotted alone time. This is a time to build self-esteem, practice thought work, get clear and get time away from distractions. I find that my mind creates incredible ideas when it is allowed prolonged amounts of time in stillness and quiet. I love long drives and solo road trips, as I find that I am able to clear my head the most on these trips. When I turn off the radio and simply notice my thoughts, notice the scenery, become quiet and still, brilliant ideas come to me. Random business ideas have formed on long drives, and fulfillment, appreciation, and happiness always accompany me when I drive long distances.

Another essential component for growth (that can be characterized as time alone) is reading a book. Books are an opportunity to step away from the everyday stress of our lives and to disappear into a wonderful world where everything is possible and we can create freely without care or judgment. In *A Wise Way*, Alexi Panos describes reading as something that, for her, "instills this endless curiosity. Endless sense of wonder for the world, this endless sense of there's got to be something else and that curiosity is a gift and it's so fun. Anyone that says that they want to live an incredible life or a life of happiness or greatness they want to leave a legacy...read because there are thousands of people who have already done that and we can get their knowledge and their wisdom in a day or a week or a month...however long it takes you to read a book." I couldn't agree with her more, and that is why reading has become one of my favorite ways to experience time alone to fuel the growth portion of my life.

PRODUCTIVITY

The components that make up productivity are Career, Life Purpose, Hobbies, and Environmental Cleanliness. My hunch is that currently your career is not fulfilling your life purpose, and that is why there are two separate categories in my circle. For me, when I created this balance circle, I had just left nannying, which previously could have been considered my career life, and was clearly separate from my life purpose. I nannied for many years, and yet it was not fulfilling my life purpose. If you are to this point in the book, you have established your mission statement. Knowing what your goals are in life will help you honor your life purpose. I know that writing my book, performing public speaking, and coaching young women all fall into alignment with my purpose. Now, this can get tricky — because fulfilling your life purpose and having a stable career that covers the bills can look like very different things. Ideally we want your life purpose to pay for your bills, however that doesn't always happen right away.

This can also be super tricky, because a million paying jobs can look like "opportunities" to further your business — when they are really just hobbies. For example, at the same time that I wanted to start my coaching career, I was also getting into photography. I was making about the same amount of money coaching as I was on photo shoots. There was a point, in my twenties, that I tried to convince myself I could successfully do both. When people asked me what I did I said, "I live life to the fullest and do a bunch of odd jobs to pay the bills." Cool, that's great — and it totally could have worked, however it didn't make me happy. It wasn't getting me closer to my goals and therefore was not even remotely fulfilling. It wasn't about making enough money to get by, it was about making a difference in the lives of others in order to effectively execute my life purpose. I never finished setting up the photography website I started. I did nothing with the classes I took at the community college, or the trainings, guidebooks, and supplies I purchased. I felt guilty about it, and like a failure for walking away from something I loved, when I determined I needed to narrow my focus to coaching. That was when I realized photography was my favorite *hobby*. Coming to the realization that I did not have to abandon this thing that totally could have been a career completely, because it could be in my life as a serious hobby, felt amazing. Having a hobby or several hobbies is an awesome way to allot time for something you love without having to worry about what your efforts are worth monetarily, or putting pressure on yourself to sell these goods. It can also be an important creative outlet to explore other areas of life you enjoy, or in the case of photography, explore your environment.

Speaking of environment! Environmental cleanliness refers to your living space and how often you spend time organizing. It is essential for your well-being that you live in a space that is clean and free of clutter. It is also important that you maintain an environment that you enjoy and inspires you. My house was a mess for years. My basement and garage were filled with furniture, and boxes upon boxes of stuff — all shit I did not need or want, but somehow I think I expected having all that stuff would bring me happiness. Once I began intensely purging, I was able to make room for things I really enjoyed in my space. It is essential that you surround yourself with meaningful items that bring you joy. I find that if I do a deep clean biweekly, and tidy as I go, I am able to successfully maintain a healthy environment.

HEALTH

Health is essential to restoring and maintaining balance in your life. Health includes sleep, nutrition, exercise, and yoga/stretching. Sleep is absolutely essential for healthy living. I noticed after focusing on maintaining regular sleep, of at least eight hours a night, that I woke up feeling full of energy and completely refreshed. This was not something I have ever been accustomed to. Even as a young child, my parents had to wake me every morning on Christmas morning...even knowing a million presents were in the next room just waiting for me to play with wasn't enough to wake this sleeping beauty.

Nutrition and diet are essential in order to fuel your body. Working out consists of elevating your heart rate for at least thirty minutes. Exercise is absolutely essential for one's health and optimal brain function. Yoga and stretching are not part of exercise, because even if you are attending the most intense yoga classes, I have found that it is not a substitute for cardio activity. Yoga and stretching has been life-changing for me. I have more mental clarity than ever before. I am able to move in ways I never knew possible, and I have felt muscle strength become increasingly better over the last few years of attending consistent yoga classes.

When you look at this circle there are imaginary tick marks from one to ten on each piece of the pie. Your goal is for everything to be at a five. Ideally nothing should below a five or above a five. After my dad died, my balance circle looked like this.

Relationships

Growth

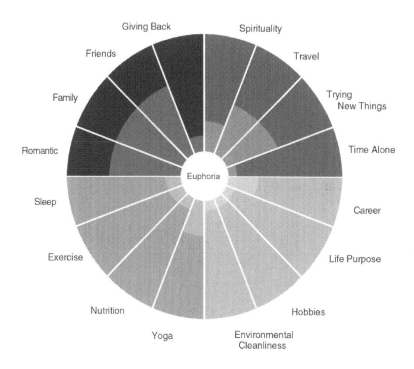

Giving Back

Spirituality

Friends

Travel

Family

Trying
New Things

Romantic

Time Alone

Sleep

Euphoria

Career

Exercise

Life Purpose

Nutrition

Hobbies

Yoga

Environmental
Cleanliness

Health

Productivity

You can see I was completely out of balance. Before considering the areas of my life that needed to be adjusted, it was important for me to consider how I was motivated. In order to do that, I needed to look over how I had accomplished goals in the past. Below, I have listed five achievements, and next to those, I listed how I was motivated to achieve my goal. I would like you to do the same with your own accomplishments.

Five accomplishments:

1. Running for STUCO president — self

2. Winning awards at HS ceremony — self

3. Officiating my friends' wedding — accountability

4. Write a book — accountability

5. Launching business — accountability

When I consider some of my major accomplishments, and how I was motivated to achieve my goals, I realized that in some cases my personal drive for success was enough to achieve my goal. In other cases, it was essential for me to have a way (or a third party) to hold myself accountable. Running for student council president and winning awards in high school were pretty easy and straightforward goals. I knew that all I had to do was play three sports and I would at least win one award at the ceremony. I knew that all I had to do to run for student council president was write a speech and present it on a certain day before the student body. In the case of writing a book and launching my business, those achievements were not as straightforward, the road map was not laid out before me, and I had spent years on my own attempting to accomplish those goals with no success. In the case of my first book, I know for a fact I absolutely could not have accomplished that goal had it not been for my publisher. I tried desperately to back out of publishing my first book, for fear that it wasn't ready, and I am confident that had it not been for my publisher pressing the release button on my book for me, I would not have released it. I know in the case of the wedding ceremony, I made a commitment to my friends and thus being motivated to keep my word to them enabled me to be held accountable.

Now it's your turn. Let's uncover what motivates you! Name five accomplishments in your lifetime and think of what helped you to achieve your goal.

Five accomplishments:

1.

2.

3.

4.

5.

Perfect. Now I want you to think for a minute...were these accomplishments easily laid out? Were the requirements clear, as in what is needed for a college diploma, or did they require a lot of trial and error and a process that was completely foreign and difficult for you to accomplish?

Once I laid out my balance circle and became aware of the areas that needed my attention and I was clear on how I become motivated to accomplish a goal I was ready to get started.

Areas that needed improvement

Giving back

Time alone

Life purpose

Hobbies

Environmental cleanliness

Exercise

Nutrition

Sleep

It was clear that time and energy would be taken away for the amount I was spending in the relationship category. That was not going to be difficult, since all of that was out of balance as a result of my father's death. So, as I looked at this, I decided to make small strides in balancing.

Otherwise, I readily could have prompted change-over-whelm, cue footage of me huddled in the corner of my room in the fetal position. I determined an easy way to give back and help with environmental cleanliness was to begin to purge belongings. Over the next six months, I donated countless truckfuls of furniture. I had many things sold at consignment shops. I donated bags and carloads of items to Goodwill. The way I continue to maintain environmental cleanliness is by donating at least one bag of items I am not madly in love with, each month, to Goodwill.

As soon as I called my publisher back, and determined I would start to write my book, even though I was dealing with the death of my father, I began to live out my life purpose. Knowing that accountability is a helpful motivator for me, I purchased a Jawbone device that I wore on my wrist to help monitor my sleep. I was able to keep track of my sleep patterns and make adjustments as needed.

There are many ways to spend time alone. I determined this year that I wished to incorporate more meditation into my weekly life, and therefore took amping up my alone time as an opportunity to meditate. I began following a thirty-day guided meditation program that I did after waking up each morning. Oh — and let's not forget — I purchased and read around twenty books during that time.

A few months before my dad passed away, I purchased an annual membership to a yoga studio nearby. Once I determined that I wanted to increase the amount of time I was spending on exercise, I decided to challenge myself to three cardio workout classes each week for a whole month. I told family and friends about it to help hold me accountable and that was a success!

Lastly, after seeing so many doctors, coaches, and guidance in regards to weight loss help, I had an overwhelming amount of blood work and tests run on my body. I learned that my body had gluten and dairy sensitivities as a result of the testing. Therefore, once I determined I wanted to pay more attention to my nutrition, I knew exactly where to begin.

My relationships were all ranked incredibly high. Even before my father passed, I was dedicating far too much of my time on my relationships with others. I would drop anything on my schedule that was set aside as time for myself, my career, goals, and well-being — for the sake of others. Then naturally, when I felt as though my friends or family were not respecting my time, schedule, or work efforts, I would become upset, offended, and beyond angry. I see now that of course they were not respecting my time, but I was expecting them to do so in spite of the fact that I was not respecting my time. By pushing workouts, time I had allotted to clean, organize, cook, work, write, or simply be alone, I was telling myself that my needs mattered less than the needs of others. In turn, that message was being conveyed to those I was dropping everything for as well.

After my dad passed, I was no longer given the option to focus on my family. My mom was traveling, my brother had retreated, and my dad was gone. My friends were unbelievable. It's amazing how something like death can truly bring to light the incredible individuals you have in your life. Sometimes it also becomes piercingly obvious who *isn't* there, and unfortunately sometimes it's the ones we expect to be. I made it a point to spend as much energy as possible on the friends that showed up, went above and beyond. I took the observation of the ones who didn't as a gift. When people show you who they really are...listen. Unfortunately, I waited far too long to distance myself from certain individuals in my life who needed to go. I spent too much time making excuses for their behavior, and ultimately forgiving them even when they did not ask for forgiveness. I learned this year that it is acceptable to give myself permission to not put more energy into someone than they are willing to give me in return. That is what friendship is all about. It is a give and take.

When hardship occurs, it is easy to focus on hurt feelings attributed to the individuals you thought would show up that don't — but I encourage you to instead embrace all the individuals that come out of the woodwork and surprise you. I had friends bringing meals, organizing get-togethers, and showing up more than I could have ever expected. I received an outpouring of love and support, unlike I had ever felt before. My friends provided me with the strength I needed to keep going, and to work to achieve my dreams. It was understandable, as a result of the circumstance, that the amount of time I was dedicating to my relationships to be greater than average. You will notice that these categories can shift — even day-to-day, month-to-month depending on your goals — which can alter how you would rank each category. And all of that is natural and healthy. One month you may be spending more time at work, maybe to work towards a promotion, so that you can have more money to take your family on a vacation. Maybe one month you are doing a workout challenge, and spending more time at the gym than normal. All of that is part of healthy balance and what occurs in our life. The purpose of this wheel is awareness, and recognizing areas you are not giving any or little attention, and acknowledging areas to which you may be giving too much energy.

Now it is your turn! Complete the balance circle on the following page and write down five areas you need to work on along with an easy way to implement that change.

Relationships

Growth

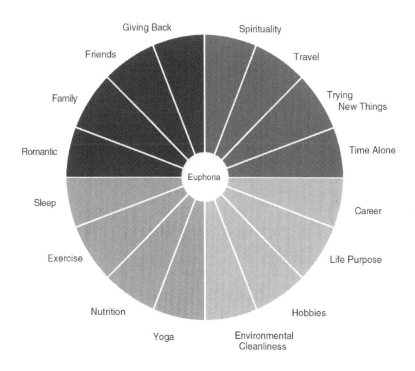

Health

Productivity

Areas to adjust — ways to implement that change:

1.

2.

3.

4.

5.

ex. 1. Yoga/stretching-join a challenge or create your own

ex 2. Sleep-buy a device and begin recording your sleep

If you would like suggestions on ways to help balance a category, go to www.StephGoldLifeCoach.com and click on the button that says "Dreamers" for free detailed suggestions of ways to more effectively implement your current trouble areas in your life!

NOTES

NOTES

CHAPTER 5

OH WAIT, MY WORK IS NOT OVER?

*There will come a time when you believe every-
thing is finished; that will be the beginning.*

LOUIS L'AMOUR

After my dad passed away, I spent the next few months reevaluating and attempting to piece my life back together. I had spent so much time focused on my family it was hard to know another way. Just as I finally mustered up the courage to pursue the life of my dreams and make my mark on the world, then my life came crashing down in an instant. I searched desperately to find signs to show he was still with me. My grandmother's death had been so magical for me, as I described. It was a spiritual awakening for me, and a moment in my life that confirmed my belief and restored my hope. Having experienced the ugly, difficult side of death in my father's passing, you can understand my desire for a sign from him. I was desperate to hear from him and know he was all right. I thought for sure the second he could give me a sign, he would.

Weeks had gone by since he died, and I hadn't heard or seen a thing. I was not feeling the presence of him, the way I had with my grandmother right after she passed — and I'll admit I was beginning to lose hope that I ever would. I was upset and surprised that I couldn't feel him the way I could Gram. Soon after his passing, I received a call that the 1947 Cadillac my father had been restoring was ready to go to upholstery. My father had been restoring this car for years. For the last few I had been working as a liaison between the technicians and my father. My dad knew exactly what he wanted down to every last detail. We had a rendering made of the interior, so that my dad would have a positive distraction from his illness. By the time the car was ready for interior, Dad was already gone. It became my passion and mission to make sure that car was completed to my father's standards, and that everything looked exactly as he had wanted. I bought a ticket and flew out to California to meet the shop guys and pick out the interior. I can still recall how emotional this trip was for me. I journeyed alone within a month of losing my father. When I arrived at the rental car place, I stood at the desk where they told me they had two cars left. They could loan me a sports car or a sedan. I told them the sedan would do just fine. Just then, a small family walked up to the counter, and I heard the man inform them that the only car left was a sports car that would not fit their family's needs. I immediately asked that they switch and give me the sports car so that the family could take the sedan. They offered me a major discount for my generosity, and handed me the keys. As I walked outside, I nearly began to cry. The sports car was a Corvette, which had been my father's favorite car. My father had collected Corvettes ever since I was a baby. We always had at least two, and I know there were years we had as many as five. It was my sign. I knew right then and there that my father was with me.

I had decided that instead of staying at a cheap motel by the car shop, that I would stay in the mountains of San Bernardino. It was a place I had never visited, and of course I was still following my desire to try new things. The drive was unlike anything I have ever seen. The views on top of the mountain were absolutely breathtaking. I walked into the hotel and was immediately upgraded to a suite — for no reason. The next day, everything went to plan. I laid out exactly what my father wanted, and picked out the interior of his car.

Shortly after his passing, I also determined I would give writing my first book another try. The majority of my writing took place in April, my family decided to travel to our vacation home in Scottsdale, Arizona, which would provide a refreshing get away from the city in which we lived and the house we grew up in that was filled with the memory of my father's illness.

My brother and I decided to drive to Arizona while my mom flew. On the drive out, my brother was determined not to stop to sleep. I am super easy-going, so I was up for whatever. We only stopped for food and gas on our 23-hour adventure across the country. It was right around sunset the first time we were passed by an old man flying down the highway in a baby-blue 1973 corvette. He flew past in an instant, and my brother and I turned to one another and I said, "Did you just see that?" He said, "Weird...right? That was Dad's favorite car." I smiled and agreed. We continued on our journey, and about an hour later, the same car went flying past us again. We both laughed and said, "I wonder where he is going?" We stopped only for gas, food, and to let our dogs out — and ventured back on the road. Hours and another state's worth of road under way, and sure enough, that old man passed us again. At this point it was early in the morning, say 1 or 2 a.m., and it was beginning to make less and less logical sense that somehow this man was repeatedly passing us on the highway. Were we going to the same place? Was he too only stopping for gas and food? How were we not seeing one another, with the exception of his passing us? Call it what you want. Think what you will. But according to my brother and I, our father sends us signs in the form of cars.

May was a crazy month, as I was working diligently to make sure all the details of my father's celebration of life party were in order. I was putting a lot of pressure on myself to make sure everything was up to his standards. I decided to give a speech to welcome everyone. I also put together many photo boards and a slideshow. A lot of effort was required on my part to make sure the evening was up to my father's standards. I was happy to put all the effort forth, of course, however there was one tiny problem — my book was scheduled to launch the week before the party, and my mom was cruising the islands with my uncle. I was on my own — and I was feeling the stress. I called my publisher and begged for more time. I explained how insane my life was and how I needed a few more weeks to make my book perfect. My publisher wasn't buying my excuses, and pushed me to publish. I published my book — and a week after, we had the celebration. Both were a huge success. We invited hundreds of people from his past. Grade school, high school, college, fraternity brothers, coworkers, neighbors, friends, and so many more were in attendance. We found the perfect band, food, décor, photographer, and other wildly perfect entertainment. My dad was so full of life and loved people living in their element. We hired everything from a bagpiper to an Elvis impersonator. The night was amazing. My book was an international #1 best seller in its first few days of being released.

I was over the moon and ready to develop my business plan, and begin its execution. Later that month, I was invited to attend an event at my publisher's house. It was a strategy meeting to help launch my business. The room was filled with intelligent minds and the woman leading the discussion was a marketing genius. At the end of the weekend I was offered an opportunity to join a year-long mentorship. The ticket price was terrifying — and for sure the most expensive thing I would have ever bought to date. I remember feeling nervous and completely out of touch with my gut feelings. I was relying on my gut to make this massive decision for me, and I couldn't feel a thing. I was offered a massive discount if I signed up on the spot. I felt like I needed to talk to my mom. I needed her approval. But how much was my mom's opinion really worth? I knew that if I didn't sign in that instance that there was great potential for my mom to talk me out of it.

When you feel resistance to something it can feel like butterflies, nervousness, anxiety, fear, goosebumps. These are words we use to describe positive experiences and negative experiences alike — but the truth is inside our bodies they can actually feel very similar, making it super confusing and hard to know the way. One thing I have learned from Lori Harder, as she teaches in her video called "Why We Can't Get to Our Goals," is this, "Resistance is usually telling us where we need to go. Follow the resistance because a lot of times that is exactly where your answer lies. When you are feeling things coming up on why you don't want to do something or you are feeling anxious or nervous about things, often times that is because that is exactly where you need to go where all your answers lie your joy will lie."

Ultimately, I knew in my heart that as a result of accountability and mentorship I had a book. (The same book that, prior to signing with my publisher, took my five years of spinning my wheels and getting me nowhere.) I knew that if I signed, I would have a much better chance of reaching my goal in a reasonable amount of time than if I attempted this venture alone. I could probably get to my end goal on my own, but who knows how long it would take me — or what excuses I might disguise as reasons to bail or detour on my journey. I decided in that moment, sitting in the living room of my mentor's home, that I had to sign up.

This time I couldn't ask my mom for permission, I had to take this leap of faith on my own — and I had to give this business everything I had *now*.

The moment I signed was a huge moment for me. It was the moment I took my life into my own hands and made my destiny my mission. If my business was going to be a success, it would be because of me. If it failed, it would be because of me. I sat and bawled hysterically as I signed those documents, because in that moment I knew I was on my own.

I spent the summer preparing my manuscript for print. During that time, I also did some goal setting and created a vision board. I put up a picture of a girl paddleboarding. I wrote that I wanted to officiate a wedding. I think this was super important to me because I had given so many eulogies in recent years that I wanted to officiate a joyous ceremony. I wrote down that I wanted to write a second book. And the last memorable goal I set was to have my first retreat. I set my vision board aside and to be honest didn't think too much of it. I began practicing gratitude daily and kept a journal. I continued my mission of trying new things and continuing to put myself out there and step outside my comfort zone. In July, I accepted a challenge at my yoga studio to complete. It was nineteen yoga classes in thirty days. Completing the challenge not only felt amazing, but it expanded my knowledge of the practice of yoga and I could feel such a transformation in such a short amount of time. I realized the importance of consistency to truly feel the benefits of anything you are doing or trying.

I explained in Chapter 1 how that one August in my year of new things, I traveled to Florida for a bachelorette party, and decided to go paddleboarding. My instructor was Pam, who I described in detail. That adventure turned out to be life-changing and completely meant to be. I now partner with Pam for annual retreats. She is a great friend, and a wonderful yoga instructor and guide. I came home from the bachelorette party and by that time wedding season was in full force. I had four weddings to attend in a two-month period of time. Upon my return, and much to my surprise, I was asked to officiate a wedding for my dear friends, Calli and Greg. This was a surprise, not only because it was something I had never done before, but also because my friendship with this couple was fairly new. I had met them only a couple years prior but had grown super close in a short amount of time. Calli is the type of friend that wears her heart on her sleeve, she is beyond loyal, and honestly one of the most pure and genuine individuals I have ever met. Greg is the most accepting, forgiving, compassionate, and loyal friend anyone could ask for. This couple's love is so strong and present when you are in their company that you can't help but want to be around them. Their love is the type of love you witness and wish for yourself. They are the most beautiful couple and as honored as I was to be asked, I hesitated.

Even though I had totally just added it to my vision board and knew it was something I wanted to do, I was terrified. What if I didn't do their love justice? What if I didn't know what I was doing? What if I found a way to mess up their perfectly, flawless day? Eventually, I got over my fear and accepted the honor, and thank goodness I did. Marrying two of my best friends was by far one of the coolest things I have ever had the pleasure of doing. I learned and grew so much through the process. It was truly the most beautiful event I have ever been a part of, not to mention how it immensely strengthened my bond with this amazing couple. This event was by far a highlight of my life. If you are keeping score, two out of the top four items of the vision board I created were crossed off in just a couple months' time...manifesting your dreams anyone?

In November, after the fourth wedding, my family traveled to Arizona over my birthday. The night before I turned twenty-nine, I decided to climb a mountain by myself and reflect on the past year. I wanted to go alone. I felt a strong desire for quiet, to be with my thoughts, and to have some peace of mind. Not long after I began walking, I felt a writer's moment coming on. I decided to keep walking and ask Siri to type. I requested that Siri open a new note for me as continued to walk, and her response was, "This is about YOU, not me." No joke...wow, Siri...profound and true. (I love when life throws little surprises my way.) So I stopped for a moment to type. I was realizing as I climbed on what happened to be the last day of my twenty-eighth year, that if things in life go to plan, the truth about life is that the only constant in our lives from birth to death is going to be ourselves. This of course means we will be spending a lot of time with ourselves and life will be a lot easier the sooner we can get on board with loving ourselves. Byron Katie says,

"It is not your job to like me. It's mine."

The hike allowed me to reflect on the journey that had been the past year of my life. I contemplated the extreme highs and lows the previous 365 days had bestowed upon me. The loss of my father was the most pain I had ever experienced in my life. The birth of my book, a longtime dream of mine, was the proudest I have ever felt of an accomplishment. The hike became more physically demanding, and I noticed my thoughts. I considered stopping halfway up the mountain and turning around, because who would know? Well, I would know, and I was the only person that mattered, because this was a goal I had set for myself and not for anyone else. I walked on and traded the "let's give up" thought for the "let's push through, I've got this" one instead. As the hike grew more difficult, I lost my way on the path. I decided to look up and keep going. I became short of breath and began thinking things like, "This is stupid, it doesn't matter if I reach the top, I should just turn around," and, "I've gone so far already, this in it of itself is an accomplishment." Those thoughts wouldn't get me to the top, so I replaced them with a three phrase mantra: "be patient, be present, you will get to the top." I continued to repeat my mantra, and before I knew it, I had indeed reached the top. I reached the top, though not on the assigned path, not taking the way laid out for me — and that was all right, because I was still at the top, exactly where I wanted to be. The way I treated myself allowed me to accomplish my goal. I remained standing at the top as I watched the sunset. I witnessed the most beautiful oranges, reds, pinks, and even purples as the sun slowly retreated. I will always recall the sun setting on my twenty-eighth birthday, and that is a memory I would never have had if I had stopped. An interesting fact is that the mountain I hiked that day is called "Lone Mountain" — how fitting.

I learned this year the true importance of challenging oneself. You are capable of so much more than you realize. I also realized that you'll never stop working and it will never be effortless. Life is about constantly evolving and changing. It is essential that we continue to grow and evolve... what, disappointed? Oh wait, my work's not over? I hate to burst your bubble, but if you are feeling high as a kite and ready to take on the world fearlessly now, sit down I have some news for you. The growth is *never* over. The key is to *never* stop learning and evolving. The act of integrating new things into our lives should be an active part of your weekly, if not daily life.

Personal development is also necessary — for the brightest and best continue to attend conferences, speakers series, join groups, mentorships, accountability programs and are linking arms with like-minded individuals. I have been taking regular yoga classes from a studio near me for a little over a year. I have participated in three challenges at my studio and I just signed up for a four-day intensive retreat in Newport Beach. When you start to become good at something, don't settle for mediocre, push yourself toward greatness.

We have identified your skills, established your ideal legacy, written your mission statement, exposed your excuses and what you will use to continue to live safely without having to dive into fear (keep yourself small), we know what motivates you so we can support your journey...*now we are ready!*

Ok, awesome — we know exactly what we are great at, we know exactly how we want to be remembered, now let's brainstorm the ways we can combine our gifts with our desired legacy, and create some ideal life careers.

I like a few options, so you can play around with what feels the most freeing. Also, you may find along your journey as you continue to gather ideas from the universe throughout your daily life that these ideas can be combined and utilized in ways you did not initially see...ex. speaker, writer, photographer (distraction or opportunity), life coaching, t-shirt idea, journal idea, camp idea, greeting card idea... easy to have a lot of ideas and the beautiful thing is you may choose to do those things or find ways to incorporate them into your life at some point. To get started it is essential to narrow your focus and get started in a direction!

We discussed the difference between a distraction and an opportunity. An opportunity is in complete alignment with your goal. Remember how earlier I described how, years ago, I wanted to coach middle school girls — and then I was offered a nanny job that comprised the care of three girls who were in middle school? It was close, but ultimately it wasn't a fit, and was simply a distraction. You'll know an opportunity the second you land on it, because it will be in complete alignment with what you are looking for. It may be easy to worry that a job opportunity this similar may not come along, so you take a close one — but the truth is that it wasn't an opportunity, it was simply a distraction. I watched a video of Jenna Philips Ballard and her explanation of this was so helpful to me. She said, "If an experience seems like it's almost ideal for us to actually fulfill our dreams, but it's not quite ideal, it's a distraction... So if you are currently in a job that you cannot stand, but then your boss comes to you offers you a raise so you can stay a little bit longer, that's a distraction, it's not an opportunity...leap and the net will appear, trust that the universe will provide for you exactly what you need for you to fulfill your purpose, so when an opportunity does arise, pause, look at it. Ask yourself, is this bringing me closer to my vision? Is this in alignment with my dreams? Is this going to forward me so that I am living my purpose? And if the answer is no to any one of those questions, it is not an opportunity, it is a distraction, and allow yourself to say no to that because when we say no, we are actually saying yes to something bigger." So when an offer comes, and you are trying to determine whether it is an opportunity or distraction, be sure to ask yourself, "Is this in complete alignment with my purpose?"

Understanding the difference between your life purpose and a hobby is an essential part in aiding you in the distinction of distraction vs. opportunity. I totally could have had a photography business, and I even started creating a website, bought trainings, and took classes at the local community college. Which was totally and completely fine for me to do, as long as I recognized it as a hobby and not a business. In order to be successful, it was essential that I become very clear on what I did for a living so that others could become very clear on what they were buying from me. I had a coaching website and a photography website, and it was at that point that I asked myself, "What legacy do I want to leave?" I reminded myself of my mission statement and decided to never fully launch the photography business.

The universe has a funny way of making you work for what you really want. Once I knew confidently and wasn't going to let my excuse of my father's illness stand in my way any longer, I quit my job, signed on with my publisher and began writing — then my father died. I could have easily made his death my new excuse not to write my book. I also could have taken it as a "sign" that I wasn't meant to write my book at that time. The universe wasn't giving me a sign to stop writing, or not to write, but instead was giving me an opportunity to show the world how badly I really wanted it. I began writing this second book less than a year after my first. I started this writing journey around the holidays, and ran into some depression around that time with the absence of my father for the first time — and then his birthday hit in January. I noticed around Thanksgiving that I was beginning to consume alcohol more than usual. Wedding season contributed, of course, but this was different. I was noticing that once I started drinking, I was consuming in excess as if to mask my sadness. Also, alcohol produces dopamine in our brains, and dopamine is highly addictive, as can alcohol be. Drinking actually made me happier as a result of the dopamine I was receiving, but I was starting to become less productive, as I was experiencing intense hangovers followed by major anxiety and depression episodes that were seeming to last for days after these crazy karaoke nights.

I determined that I was indeed using alcohol to mask my sadness — and decided that was not the way I wanted to cope, nor did I want my clients to cope in that manner. Thus, I determined I would allow myself three drinks a week. I decided that this would allow for a glass of wine with my mom on occasion, a margarita with the girls, or I could save all three drinks for a Saturday wedding or fun event. It was a way for me to adjust my consumption to a healthy balance without feeling deprived or like I would constantly have to say "no" all the time. I will admit I fully adopted this concept months ago. At first, I would keep track and mark the nights I had a drink, to confirm I was only having three a week. Now I can say that I successfully go week after week without consuming at all, and don't think twice about it.

I was never one to drink alone, even a glass a wine, I never saw the point. My issue was after a few drinks, and feeling so happy with friends, I was using it in lieu of real happiness (dopamine...the quick happiness fix that is incredibly addicting). The point is self-awareness is so key in determining what in your life is no longer serving you. You could make a case either way, say, *Well, I don't really have a problem because I don't drink on my own and I only get too drunk on occasion and always take cabs*. Ok cool — but is it serving you? Is it helping you reach your goals? What are you gaining from participating in that action? Is this action propelling you toward your goal and helping you live your purpose? Once I realized how counterproductive the momentary enjoyment of drinking was, I made an adjustment. Recognizing what is serving you and no longer serving you and making adjustments accordingly is key. Don't spend time being hard on yourself just learn from it and move on.

During the writing of my second book, there was a week I fell behind my writing deadlines due to holiday depression and missing my father. I was a chapter and day away from submitting my first draft to my editor, and that's when my hard drive on my computer crashed. For two days, I wandered around not knowing if I had lost everything. I had come to grips with the fact that it might all be gone. I determined that even if I lost everything, I would spend a week rewriting everything I could recall and I would make the content even better than before. After I came to the conclusion that I was writing this book no matter what, it was time for the moment of truth. I learned that my hard drive crashed — and I would have lost everything had I not backed it up before the crash. Even though I backed it up, I was still unsure of the backup's success since I backed it while the hard drive was failing. Regardless, the point is, shit will absolutely happen. You can choose to take it as a "sign" that you aren't meant to do something and use that excuse — or you can choose to see it as a way of helping you show the world how determined you truly are! You will be super close to success and everything will be going to plan — until all of sudden something doesn't, and you are forced to display to the universe how badly you want to succeed. Expect it, because life has a crazy way of keeping us on our toes and making us work for the things we really want.

Since we know the day will come when you feel like giving up entirely, let's create a playlist you will listen to on those days (after you've allowed yourself to wallow for a hot second). I will share some of the songs on my playlist with you...they are get it girl, this is my anthem, belt it from your lungs, windows down type songs.

"I'm A Survivor" (Destiny's Child)

"Alive" (Sia)

"Hold On" (Wilson Philips)

"Fight Song" (Rachel Platten)

"Me, Myself, & I" (G-Eazy x Bebe Rexha)

These songs get me pumped and allow me to get out my frustration so that I am ready to jump back on the saddle. I want you to think of a playlist. Positive songs with awesome messages that will remind you of your mission.

1.

2.

3.

4.

5.

Perfect, you are set!! You have all the tools you need.

Now, I want you to think of Pam and Morgan, who I introduced in Chapter 1. I want you to think of me and all the time I spent buying and selling excuses, the time I wasted treading water in the middle of the pool. I want you to really see yourself in five or more years if you don't choose to start implementing your passion now. Where are you at Pam or Morgan's age, at my age, or at any age if you continue to "wait for the right time?" These are super charged, more than capable, fiercely driven women who also became momentarily blinded by society and the views of others. If it can happen to them, and to me, I am confident it can happen to you. Maybe you're still with me right now because you recognize it in yourself.

So my question for you is this...

How long will you make the wrong thing "work" until it doesn't anymore? The universe will interfere if you continue to attempt to deny fate. You'll get fired, he will dump you, things you are not expecting and can't avoid will occur — and they will not make any sense to you either. You'll sit there and think, *But I was working so hard to avoid that...I did everything right...how could that have possibly have happened?* Oh right, yeah, because you don't have control over fate. Somewhere along the line you have become seriously out of touch with what you really want, and can't see it.

So after much reflection, be prepared to get it...really get it... and then expect to be offered an easy way out. You'll be able to justify completely why this time it's different, how this is not the same thing. That's when the universe is testing you... how badly do you really want this thing you say you want?

I cannot express how much my life has shifted since I said, "Yes" to my mentorship. For me, the shift has occurred not only as a result of having accountability to my mentor but also being a part of a strong network of individuals who send me love and support me on hard days, and love and celebrate me on epic days. My first experience with an accountability program was in the writing of my book. I spent five years "writing" a book, but it wasn't until I experienced an accountability program that I actually became a published author. Once I began to apply accountability to other areas of my life, I was able to see major shifts happening in such a positive way. My success with this system is what caused me to create a similar system with my clients.

I have created a community for young dreamers to develop their vision, and link arms with like-minded female pow-erhouses, while they execute their dreams. If you are a dreamer and are ready to change the world, I urge you to become clear on your vision and jump into action...the world is waiting for you!

Last exercise I swear...write down the three reasons why *now* is not only the *right* time for you to get started, but the *only* time...

1.

2.

3.

Awesome, so what are you going to do about it? Join the movement, make the decision to jump in the driver's seat of your life! Come to a retreat, or schedule a call with me! Whatever you decide to do, do not wait...no matter what NOW IS YOUR TIME!

NOTES

NOTES

ACKNOWLEDGEMENTS

Thank you to everyone who has supported me on this journey. This last year of my life has been that of the most epic growth I have ever experienced.

Thank you to my mother for always believing in me. Your strength and encouragement, this year especially, have left my heart so full of love and appreciation for you. You are my inspiration, drive, and beacon of unconditional love. Thank you endlessly for all that you do and have always done to support my dreams.

To my father, you will never know how your display of positivity has shaped me to my absolute core. There is not a day that goes by that I do not long to laugh with you again. My favorite place in the world remains on top of your shoulders. The love you gave me was enough to live off of for all of eternity.

Thank you to my friend and partner in crime. You hold many titles in my life but the one I cherish the most is brother. I prayed for you every night, I asked Santa for you every year. The world has never known someone more wanted and loved than you were even before you arrived. I am grateful for you beyond words and cherish our bond.

To my girlfriends and close female confidants-ladies, I waited my entire life to feel true friendship and I feel overwhelmingly blessed to have each and every one of you in my life. You women have been so pivotal during this time. You girls have lifted me, cried with me, laughed with me and I love you all endlessly. Thank you for your patience and words of encouragement.

Calli and Greg, officiating your wedding was such a high-light of my year. Thank you both for entrusting me with such a privilege on your special day. Lizzie, I could not love your family more. I thank you endlessly for allowing me to end my 18-year-long love of babysitting on such a high note. I cherish our friendship.

Gerard, your support and encouragement in the pursuit of my dreams have been such a true blessing in my life and throughout this year. I love and appreciate all the reassurance you have offered me on difficult days and my heart feels so incredibly full to have you in my life. I am so grateful for you and shark.

Thanks to the one that sat by me as I typed every word and never rushed me. Gizmo, you are the best companion and sweetest pup in the world. You bring me comfort and love, thank you for sticking by my side always.

Thank you to my mentor. You have pushed me far beyond my wildest dreams or expectations for one year's worth of accomplishments and in what was by far my most diffi-cult and trying emotional year, might I add. I love you and appreciate you more than words can articulate. Thank you also for creating an inspirational group whose love I can feel across many states. Order of the Plume peeps, thank you for your acceptance, love, belief, and encouragement, your ability to lift me up is unmatched. Love to you all.

Thank you to my editor, publishing team, supportive team of authors, and Angela to whom I could not have done this without. Kate, you were far more than an editor to me through this process, thank you for holding my hand and allowing me to cry on your shoulder as I faced the last ten years of my life with an open heart.

Thank you Morgan and Pam for allowing me to share your amazing stories. Also a thank you to my friend Sarah Caracciolo for your help and support!!

Thank you Ellen DeGeneres for displaying to the world acceptance and unconditional love. Thank you for making daily dance a necessity and for honoring schools and teachers who make dreams like mine a reality. Your show continues to serve as my "afternoon break" and I am forever grateful for the inspiration and encouragement you supply to the world.

I appreciate all the love, support, and encouragement I have received from family and friends. Thank you everyone who has encouraged and supported me over the years, the teachers who spent time editing every line of my papers and the strangers in passing that listened to my goal and encouraged me. I appreciate the outpouring of love and support tremendously from all those I have encountered.

ABOUT THE
AUTHOR

I graduated college with a major in Communications with
an emphasis in Human Relations and a minor, Psychology
of Leadership. I was determined and ready to help young
women. I had established that I wanted to positively impact
the lives of millions of women worldwide. I knew I wanted
to help guide women to a life filled with freedom, fulfillment, joy, and purpose. I knew I wanted to aid women in
the discovery of their best life now and to support them in
the achievement of their wildest dreams. The problem was
not the *what*, it was the *how*...

I spent the next few years after college spinning my wheels,
networking like crazy, but struggling to find a true fit for
the vehicle in which to most effectively execute my mission.
I decided to spend a lot of time on myself. I took a nine-

month life coaching training, attended countless retreats, conferences, and workshops. I grew and learned a ton but, I was not truly any closer to my dream of making a true impact in the lives of these women.

I began to coach "quarter-life crisis" groups of women, ages ranging from twenty-four to thirty-two. I found the drastic improvements in their lives and overall happiness after coaching to be incredibly fulfilling. I knew coaching was a huge asset to aiding in the ignition of mental shifts and self-discovery for these individuals. The only downside was that many years had gone by from the time they graduated to the time they came looking for coaching to solve their "unhappiness" issue. In order for them to uncover their ideal life, a lot of peeling back layers of their life since college was required. I coached breakups, switching career paths, moving across states, friendship shifts, and so on.

The "undoing" of decisions that had been made as a result of a variety of reasons; wanting to make their parents proud, worrying about money, fear of being alone or not being married before thirty...oh the horror. Regardless of the reason it was painful to constantly focus on what we were going to "undo" to help my clients achieve optimal happiness. This had me thinking...what if I could reach these women right after graduation and support them there... before there was anything to "undo"? What if I could mentor them to follow their heart, their passion and soul's journey from the beginning? Thus the birth of my retreats. There was no need to waste years of their life searching for the "right fit" as their time would be much better served creating their ideal life, now.

My retreats serve as a sanctuary for the soul, a safe place to dive deeply so that you can hear your voice clearly and uncover all the answers you desire. Your soul carries all the answers to your questions but it is difficult to hear in the commotion and confusion of so many other opinions. I have a unique style that enables me to connect with young women in a way that allows them the ability to dive deeply quickly so that they are able to move along on their path and soar. I've been there, I spent years playing small and making excuses and I wouldn't trade those years for anything because they made me an incredible bullshit detector. I did it all so that you don't have to, we can cut to the chase and determine exact steps you need to take to accomplish your goals and avoid of the unnecessary distractions and detours along the way! I am absolutely determined to help women discover the passion of their soul, their mission from the universe, as well as aid them in the execution of their mission.

THANK YOU!

Hello Beautiful Dreamer,

I have a thank you present just for you! Head over to my website, which is at www.StephGoldLifeCoach.com.

Click on the "Dreamers" button for a free workbook to go along with my book! There is also access to this workbook in the link provided in my Instagram profile: StephGold_LifeCoach.

If you are ready to dive deeper and are interested in upcoming retreats set up a Dreamer call on www.TalkToSteph.com. This free call will direct you to all the information you need about the locations and details of upcoming retreats!!

Sending so much LOVE to you Dreamers!! You will change the world!!!

LOVE YOU,
Steph Gold

difference press

Difference Press offers entrepreneurs, including life coaches, healers, consultants, and community leaders, a comprehensive solution to get their books written, published, and promoted. A boutique-style alternative to self-publishing, Difference Press boasts a fair and easy-to-understand profit structure, low-priced author copies, and author-friendly contract terms. Its founder, Dr. Angela Lauria, has been bringing to life the literary ventures of hundreds of authors-in-transformation since 1994.

LET'S MAKE A DIFFERENCE WITH YOUR BOOK
You've seen other people make a difference with a book. Now it's your turn. If you are ready to stop watching and start taking massive action, reach out.

"Yes, I'm ready!"

In a market where hundreds of thousands books are published every year and are never heard from again, all participants of The Author Incubator have bestsellers that are actively changing lives and making a difference.

In two years we've created over 134 bestselling books in a row, 90% from first-time authors. We do this by selecting the highest quality and highest potential applicants for our future programs.

Our program doesn't just teach you how to write a book—our team of coaches, developmental editors, copy editors, art directors, and marketing experts incubate you from book idea to published bestseller, ensuring that the book you create can actually make a difference in the world. Then we give you the training you need to use your book to make the difference you want to make in the world, or to create a business out of serving your readers. If you have life-or world-changing ideas or services, a servant's heart, and the willingness to do what it REALLY takes to make a difference in the world with your book, go to http://theauthorincubator.com/apply/ to complete an application for the program today.

Clarity Alchemy: When Success Is Your Only Option

by Ann Bolender

Cracking the Code: A Practical Guide to Getting You Hired

by Molly Mapes

Divorce to Divine: Becoming the Fabulous Person You Were Intended to Be

by Cynthia Claire

Facial Shift: Adjusting to an Altered Appearance

by Dawn Shaw

Finding Clarity: Design a Business You Love and Simplify Your Marketing

by Amanda H. Young

Flourish: Have It All Without Losing Yourself

by Dr. Rachel Talton

Marketing To Serve: The Entrepreneur's Guide to Marketing to Your Ideal Client and Making Money with Heart and Authenticity

by Cassie Parks

NEXT: How to Start a Successful Business That's Right for You and Your Family

by Caroline Greene

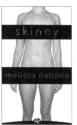

*Pain Free: How I
Released 43 Years
of Chronic Pain*

by Dottie DuParcé
(Author), John F.
Barnes (Foreword)

*Secret Bad Girl:
A Sexual Trauma
Memoir and
Resolution Guide*

by Rachael
Maddox

*Skinny: The Teen
Girl's Guide to
Making Choices,
Getting the Thin
Body You Want,
and Having the
Confidence You've
Always Dreamed Of*

by Melissa Nations

*The Aging Boomers:
Answers to Critical
Questions for You,
Your Parents and
Loved Ones*

by Frank M. Samson

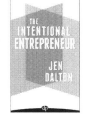

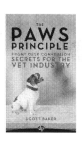

*The Incubated
Author: 10 Steps to
Start a Movement
with Your Message*

by Angela Lauria

*The Intentional
Entrepreneur: How
to Be a Noisebreaker,
Not a Noisemaker*

by Jen Dalton
(Author), Jeanine
Warisse Turner
(Foreword)

*The Paws Principle:
Front Desk
Conversion Secrets
for the Vet Industry*

by Scott Baker

*Turn the Tide:
Rise Above Toxic,
Difficult Situations
in the Workplace*

by Kathy Obear

Made in the USA
San Bernardino, CA
26 October 2016